I just completed Jim Friesen's *More Than Survivors*. It is a masterpiece. Jim does an incredible job of empowering and complementing each survivor's sense of self and creative ability to live beyond survival. He also magnifies our Creator and the power of Christ, while maintaining the focus and purpose of the book with appropriate interjections and clarifications.

—From a Survivor

Uncovering the Mystery of MPD
by James G. Friesen, Ph. D.

is also available
from your Christian bookstore
or from the publisher.

More Than Survivors

JAMES G. FRIESEN, PH.D.

THOMAS NELSON PUBLISHERS
NASHVILLE

Published by
HERE'S LIFE PUBLISHERS, INC.
P. O. Box 1576
San Bernardino, CA 92402

Cover design by Garborg Design Works

Library of Congress Cataloging-in-Publication Data
Friesen, James G.
    More than survivors : conversations with multiple-personality
clients / James G. Friesen.
        p.   cm.
    Includes bibliographical references and index.
    ISBN 0-89840-353-7
    1. Multiple personality—Patients—Interviews. 2. Multiple
personality. I. Title.
RC569.5.M8F75   1992
616.85'236—dc20   92-15157
                                        CIP

Upon the release of each new book, Here's Life Publishers sponsors the planting of a tree through Global ReLeaf™, a program of the American Forestry Association.

Scripture quotations are from *The Holy Bible: New International Version,* © 1973, 1978, 1984 by the International Bible Society. Published by Zondervan Bible Publishers, Grand Rapids, Michigan.

For More Information, Write:
L.I.F.E.—P.O. Box A399, Sydney South 2000, Australia
Campus Crusade for Christ of Canada—Box 300, Vancouver, B.C., V6C 2X3, Canada
Campus Crusade for Christ—Pearl Assurance House, 4 Temple Row, Birmingham, B2 5HG, England
Lay Institute for Evangelism—P.O. Box 8786, Auckland 3, New Zealand
Campus Crusade for Christ—P.O. Box 240, Raffles City Post Office, Singapore 9117
Great Commission Movement of Nigeria—P.O. Box 500, Jos, Plateau State Nigeria, West Africa
Campus Crusade for Christ International—100 Sunport Lane, Orlando, FL 32809, U.S.A.

*This book is dedicated to
survivors,
particularly those
whose story
has not yet been told.*

CONTENTS

People were bringing little children
to Jesus to have him touch them,
but the disciples rebuked them.
When Jesus saw this, he was indignant. He said
to them, "Let the little children come to me,
and do not hinder them,
for the kingdom of God
belongs to such as these.
I tell you the truth, anyone who will not receive
the kingdom of God
like a little child will never enter it."
And he took the children in his arms,
put his hands on them
and blessed them.

(Mark 10:13-16)

1

WAKING UP

WITH EYES not even open yet, in my very first waking moment that morning, I felt a surge of excitement. My body, worn out from teaching seminars for two days, was not exactly ready for the excitement, but my mind, making lots of noise, flashed its message to me in bright colors: "Wake up! They were splendid! People need to get that message!"

The audience had been awe-stricken! The brief seminar, in which the three "multiples" shared their stories and answered questions, was absolute dynamite! The listeners were elated, and people could hardly leave the room when the meeting ended. I would not be going back to sleep this morning, that was certain. My mind was still revving up. "You need to convey this message to a wider audience. Multiples are splendid people. They are *more* than survivors. They have grace . . . and power!"

I was not particularly happy with the work I had done as a seminar presenter. My eight hours of teaching about treatment for people with multiple personality was only a faint success compared to the overwhelmingly positive response to the two hours of teaching by the multiples.

My book had come out two weeks earlier; my seminar work was now completed, and this morning was supposed to be kick-back time. My family and I planned to spend the day at Disneyland, and I wanted to think of nothing more than how to stay dry on the water rides! Evidently, my mind had been active during that night, though, because it made a particularly important connection.

Within the first fifteen seconds of my awareness, I suddenly grasped why I enjoy working with these people—they are more than just interesting people. These people consistently cause others to say to themselves, "I am very fortunate to know someone like that." As a therapist, I look forward to being with them. As a person, I appreciate them. As a psychologist, I do not understand how they could go through such serious suffering and still retain their natural talents. As a friend, I rejoice with them when they achieve healing and wholeness.

The audience, mostly Christian professionals, had reached the same conclusion. They also found these to be remarkable, engaging people; not just because of the things they talked about, but because of the way they are—sensitive, helpful, bright and spontaneous. Their opening statements had been riveting; they answered the audience's questions with clarity, and the listeners could hardly stop expressing their appreciation. People loved them.

A MISUNDERSTOOD DIAGNOSIS

Another connection was also made during the night: It would take a *miracle* to break through the stereotype of public misperception about multiples in order to deliver the message about their splendidness. There have been movies about people with multiple personality disorder (MPD), sitcoms have picked up story lines about MPD, and many TV talk shows and radio call-ins have reflected the public's growing interest in MPD. We even see car commercials in which somebody's personalities tell each other what they like about the automobile!

Despite the increasing public awareness, the popular portrayals convey a completely inaccurate picture of these people's nature! Things keep getting slanted in the wrong direction. Multiples are routinely shown switching and being temporarily disoriented. That is the way they have always needed to cope because of the abuse they received, but being disoriented does not mean they are less effective than the rest of humanity. Quite the opposite! They are high in intelligence and creativity, and they are able to switch between personalities only because they are gifted. Many are highly productive, powerful people, and many are simply ingenious.

MPD is not a disease. It results from dissociation, a God-given coping style that gifted children learn to use to protect themselves from the effects of serious traumas. There is nothing *wrong* with these people. In fact, there is something *right* with them. They are talented enough to use that coping style. Still, particularly in the car commercial, MPD is displayed as something to joke about, and at the very least it makes MPD fair game for stereotypically degrading comments.

MPD is not schizophrenia. People with schizophrenia need antipsychotic medication to help them process daily information correctly. Otherwise their brains can randomly misdirect things. Theirs is a malady that needs to be controlled by properly monitored drugs and by environmental shaping. It is a medical condition. MPD does not result from random misdirection of brain action. Since practically all of a brain's work is sorting out information and focusing on the task at hand, the brains of multiples must be highly effective. They block painful things out of awareness, which allows the person to stay on task very well. However, because of the highly effective pain-blocking, information gets temporarily misplaced, as the multiple moves between areas of daily life. Blank spots can occur, for pain-blocking reasons, and disorientation results. These people will need no long-term medication[1] or environmental control, because when wholeness is achieved and therapy is finished, they often show up among society's highest achievers.

People with MPD do not deserve to be stigmatized for their giftedness. They did not choose to be abused—they were just able to deal with it creatively. It takes a superb person to be able to shift from one personality to another in order to deal with the traumas that led to MPD. These people are spectacular, but they keep getting presented to the public as damaged folks.

Within a few seconds of my wakefulness that "Disneyland" morning, I knew there was a lot of ground to plow. The whole field of public perception—what MPD *is* and what it *is not*—has to be plowed under, and these splendid people should do the plowing. Allowing them to speak to an audience larger than this seminar would be a step toward undoing the public's mistaken perception.

No wonder I was alert with the dawn! Presenting these people in print, creating a book in their own words, would be an opportunity to break through the prevailing stereotype. "Wake up, everybody! Take another look at MPD, everybody."

When I had received approval to let the three multiple clients present their own seminar, I gave them the right to speak openly about anything they wanted. I believed in them and I knew they would do just fine without any prompting from me. They did not let me down—in fact, they outdid anything I had expected, as the reader will find. Highlights from the seminar have been transcribed in the next four chapters.

The first book I wrote was from a therapist's perspective. Now it is time to get the clients' perspectives. The early morning message was coming in: "The new book should be called, *Conversations with Multiple Personality Clients*. There are probably a number of other splendid, dissociating people who would be willing to talk with you. Get their stories."

THE GIFT – DISSOCIATION

Dissociation is the best defense mechanism anybody can use to deal with pain. It is the instant, complete forgetting of a trauma. It effectively disconnects the person from the event. The traumatic memories are stored in alternate personalities, sometimes called "alters," where the events remain hidden from the other personalities. If dissociation is learned early in life, it becomes the preferred method of coping. Since it is the best defense, it is used all the time. Not only does it allow the person to live without awareness of pain, but the switching also can be used to stay safe—alters can be used to fit in practically anywhere, to avoid further traumas. When a system of alters develops to keep things safe, and to deal with the different tasks of a person's life, switching (dissociating) can be observed. For a fuller explanation, see my book, *Uncovering the Mystery of MPD*, chapter 2.

Most people are slow to understand that persons with multiplicity are actually gifted. Not too long ago, there was a

20-minute segment on a popular TV show which portrayed the predicament of one woman, identified as a multiple. She had been misdiagnosed as a schizophrenic and had received incorrect treatment for a number of years, *in a mental hospital!* While she was there, on anti-psychotic medication, her switching system worked well enough to gain her release, but information was being lost between her alters. The mental hospital should have been helping the alters share their information, but hospital personnel had the wrong diagnosis. The medication and treatment seemed to prevent her system from working together. While hospitalized, a stable personality evidently gained enough control to live independently, so she was discharged. But her other personalities soon started switching in again, and the stable personality was not informed of their activities. The personality system was not working together well enough to prevent her from making mistakes—mistakes she certainly would not have made with the proper diagnosis and treatment in the hospital! At the time she was *correctly* diagnosed with MPD, she was in jail for robbery! What a tragedy—misdiagnosed, mistreated, released unhealed, and then jailed for a crime that most of her personalities did not even know about!

The TV piece did a fine job on facial close-ups with her— there were unmistakable depictions of switches between personalities. When one of the personalities emerged to say that she is really a very intelligent person but most people don't believe that, my head started nodding. I said, "I believe it!"

However, I expect most viewers of that show believed she was wrong, because they had seen disorientation. That is the kind of error I hope to counter with this book. She *is* an intelligent person, or she would not have been able to develop MPD in the first place. Her giftedness has been occluded and camouflaged because of the superior coping style she is capable of!

I know some people who probably have the potential to use this gift, but fortunately for them, they have never needed to use it. Those who ended up needing the gift are the unfortunate ones. Whenever I see a person switch to a new personality, I can safely conclude that there is good news and there is bad news: The person is gifted, and the person has been traumatized. That much is practically 100 percent certain. MPD cannot develop in a person unless that person possesses a high level of intelligence and creativity.

The effective use of dissociation enables a young child to grow up innocent and free from the awful memories that would otherwise present major developmental problems. Through dissociation, the natural talents of the child are preserved, and the abuse does not destroy the child's pristine personality. When the abuse memories are healed and the inflicted damage overcome, these people can return to their natural state—gems with their luster restored. The protection of the gem is the gift!

HOW DISSOCIATION WORKS[2]

The most clearly identifiable type of dissociation is MPD. When amnesia is present, as in most people whose diagnosis is MPD, there are blank spots in the day. Paula, in chapter 9, talks about how amnesia disrupted her life. The "host" personality, the one in charge most of the time, would settle on a particular furniture arrangement, buy certain foods, buy appropriate clothing, and, since she was well into her adult life, would have no reason to keep toys around the house. It exasperated her to find that sometimes clothes had disappeared and been replaced by a whole new wardrobe (by alters who had strong ideas about apparel), food had disappeared and been replaced by junk food (by teenage alters), whole new sets of toys had been purchased and strewn about the house (by child alters), and often furniture had been rearranged during the night (by amnesic alters)! After a few episodes like this, it was not difficult to diagnose amnesia. Switching between personalities, and experiencing memory loss like Paula's, is one way dissociation works.

Other types of dissociation and partial dissociation do not include loss of time, and there may be no apparent switching. When the memories of painful events are fully hidden and do not switch in often, the emotions from the events may seep into other areas of the person's life, and become evident for no apparent reason. A particular feeling may just intrude, very strongly, with no remembered event behind it. That is another way dissociation works, and the painful memory itself may not surface, even though the memory's feelings are strongly present. Such was the case for Crystal, who was one of the seminar presenters. When she would get torpedoed by unknown feelings, it was from that kind of indirect influence of the traumatic events. The feelings needed to heal, but the event was not yet ready to switch in. As her therapy progressed, the memories were uncovered and healing came to them, but her daily life was not disorganized because of amnesia. Hers is an example of how dissociation can work differently than it does in MPD.

HIDDEN MEMORIES

A disturbing and perplexing part of MPD is the uncovering of hidden memories. By definition, dissociated memories are forgotten. When remembered, they usually are unbelievable to the dissociator. They are awful, painful, and even grotesque events that nobody wants to discover. "That didn't happen to me!" is a common response. "I must be nuts!" is another. Friends and family can be in denial too. We all would like to believe those things didn't happen, but maybe they did.

I often say, "Because it happened to another part of you, it does not feel real to you. It is a different alter's memory. As you get a better connection to that other personality, you will find whether it is true. If it is a genuine memory, it will become part of your shared memory. As the amnesia between you disappears, you will know. You're not nuts. Your brain is just working very hard to protect you from painful memories."

When a memory comes in, it is a very intense process, involving images, feelings and bodily pain. Whether the memories are of incest, physical abuse or satanic ritual abuse, they come in the same way. A person can uncover incest memories first, and the person is seriously affected. Months later, the same person can have SRA memories surface, and the painful process is identical. Dissociated memories are hidden, and it is not known exactly what they contain until they are uncovered.

No matter what their content, memories can receive healing, but it takes uncovering first. It also takes courage to go through the pain, but the healing that results is worth enduring the process.

DISPLAYING THE GIFT

Not many MPD clients are free to share their story. There is the public stereotype, the stigma, and there is the reality of the abuse, often perpetrated by relatives. It is frequently decided to keep the abuse out of the public eye—because of complications for the family.[3] On rare occasions multiples will tell their story, but most of the time they only can do so anonymously.[4]

Since the release of my first book, I have met a number of multiples, in treatment with other therapists, who have rarely had an opportunity to speak openly. The majority of this book will be devoted to letting them do just that. Please let me emphasize that during therapy, and even without therapy, their splendid traits are evident, but particularly at the conclusion of treatment, their giftedness is hard to miss. It is like a powerful engine that gets tuned up during therapy, so the power can become fully available. Of the nine featured multiples in this book, four can be considered "fully fused," and all nine have endearing, lovely characteristics.

As I began to ask therapists if they knew multiples who would be willing to tell their story here, I was a little surprised to find how many *are* willing to share, provided their identity will be protected. There were just too many for one book, but I have settled on interviewing seven who received treatment from other therapists, from all over the country. I know that Southern California has the "reputation" of being a place for unbelievable things, but please consider this book to be based on people from across the country. Seven other therapists from six other states were involved, and none of the people featured knew each other. These peoples' stories overlap in quite a few areas, but I have chosen to focus on different aspects of their lives, highlighted in the conversations we had. The next four chapters will help you sense why the audience responded to the seminar with so much enthusiasm.

2

CRYSTAL:
Receiving
Cleansing

IT WAS A moment to relish. The seminar was just about to begin. The three people involved had been forbidden early in their lives to tell their secrets, and they had remained silent for many years. Nobody would forbid them this time. They were going to share some very personal things, including what had helped or hadn't helped in therapy. Not many audiences would be able to believe them, but at least today, their integrity would be honored. Although they have seldom been allowed to share their thoughts about life and about therapy, this time they have been sought out to *teach therapists about life!*

The room filled up and more chairs had to be brought in. Willie Marie had set up her massive display of handmade dolls and stuffed bears. Newheart had her artwork close by, ready to circulate the pieces. Crystal engaged in animated conversation. I tested microphones and set up the overhead projector.

I introduced myself first, and added that this is the two-hour seminar, led by multiples.

Jim: Welcome. We are going to be talking with three survivors. You will have a chance to ask them some questions after they each have shared a little about their experiences. I have not told them what to talk about, and really do not know what they are going to say! We are especially glad to welcome Pearl, a therapist from another state, and her client Newheart, who will be one of the presenters.

This meeting is an open forum, and I'm certain we are in for an interesting, informative time. Only one rule will need to be enforced when asking questions: Don't challenge or confront the presenters, or you will be asked to leave. It is extremely important that these three receive support here as they risk opening themselves up in a very personal way. These three individuals have suffered. Yet God has stayed with them and they are in a position now where they can talk about their suffering more openly. I think you will find, as I have, that they are remarkable people. By using dissociation they have maintained their appealing traits.

So let's start with Crystal. I'll just kind of kick back, and let you people take over!

Crystal: Hi! It's kind of empowering to sit up here and know that I can shoo you guys off, if I want to! [Laughs spring up all around the room.]

I want to start by telling you a little bit about my background, just to bring you up to speed as to where I am right now with therapy, and how I got there, and even why it was neat for me to come here. Jim did not come and ask me to be here. He's not exploiting us. The opportunity for me to be able to speak, and tell the truth about ritual abuse, and about what Jesus has done in my life—that was why I wanted to come.

One Scripture has been important to me in my healing. When people asked me why it was so important for me to go through the horrifying memories, I could respond with, "You shall know the truth and it will set you free" (John 8:32). And I figured that the more people who know the truth, the more people will be set free. So it is a neat opportunity to be here.

Just a little overview of where I was when I came to Jim. All I knew, and all I remembered from my childhood, was that when I was only one and a half years old, my mother shot my father. It happened in our driveway, and it was officially called an accident. That's how things started out for me.

My mom married three times by the time I was nine. As a kid I had them numbered—my first father, my second father, and then her third husband. I never considered him my father. I had such hatred for him. I became the black sheep of the family because of that, and I was always considered the troublemaker.

But I became a Christian. I went through a troubled, rebellious childhood and got into all those things that people do. During my growing-up years, my mother was an alcoholic—I had remembered that much when I came to Jim! Those things were enough to last me through more than a year of therapy. My mother wasn't the type who only had a little too much to drink— she would get completely incoherent. She would talk about barring the windows to save the children, because the redcoats were coming and were smashing the pillars in our driveway.

I grew up with a lot of shame; I felt like the pauper's daughter. While everybody else was in the king's palace enjoying a feast, I was only the kid of the pauper. I was full of shame, and I knew that everybody looked at me with disdain; I was cast out and never allowed to come in. With each group of memories that comes in for me, God takes me into His arms and brings healing to me, and that sense of shame grows less and less.

I was in therapy for a year before the memories started coming. I had no memory at all of the abuse at home, or of the ritual abuse. When the first memories started coming back, I got just little pieces. It wasn't the full thing. I remembered being in a room with my mother's third husband. He started talking to me about sex, "You should know about this," and all that. That was as much as I could remember right then.

For my first memory work session with Jim, I asked my pastor to be there with me. It was important to me to have spiritual guidance. It was the way I had been brought up. Jim always was more than willing to allow me that. If any of you have ever seen anybody directly after open heart surgery, that's the best picture I can give you. It felt like somebody had just cut my ribs open, and then started digging for all the disease and the tumor, to bring it all out, and it was excruciatingly painful. I cried through the whole thing.

Being able to pray before, during, and after my sessions has been a tremendous blessing. I have seen God speak through the people praying for me, and I have felt His spirit move. It is the difference between walking into your doctor's office and *hoping* all will work out, or being able to choose the Great Physician as your doctor and knowing it will all work together for good. I felt His love and His covering. By praying, we allow God to take charge, not us. He leads us and directs us, and I always am amazed at His work and at His love for me. He intimately knows every part of my mind, my soul and my heart, and He can take my shattered heart and make it whole.

The minute I walked out after recalling my first memory of being abused at home—it didn't involve the ritual abuse—I said to myself, "You've made this all up! It didn't really happen, and now what are you going to do?" I was confused. But it's been a year and a half now, and I know I didn't make it up. I wish I had.

That was how it started for me. When the memories first started coming, I couldn't control it. I didn't know how to stop them. When I was at home they kept flooding back at full speed. I got so depressed that I became suicidal. I didn't see any reason to go on, even though I had been a Christian, working for my church and being involved in ministry for about ten years. I thought, "God, you put me on this earth just to watch me squirm on the ground like a worm, and what's the point of it?"

What I see now, as I look back, is that as each group of memories came up, the pain would take over and sort of cover every other part of me. That one part of me didn't see any reason to live because she was in so much pain and she didn't have any comfort, or any hope, or any peace. She didn't know Jesus. So each time I've had a new group of memories, I've had to go through the process again, and I've learned a little better to control them.

Sometimes I tell myself, "Just put one foot on the floor. Just stand up. Just walk across the room." I need to get away from the memories until I can get to my therapy appointment where we can deal with them. It's really been helpful for me there.

Sometimes I have a session with two people. One thing that had comforted me is that one of my friends who is there for me has been a survivor also. Just to know that somebody else there has been through it, and knows what it's like has been a tremendous help! You can't possibly begin to understand unless you've been through it. She's there, and she can affirm me.

That's something I didn't get from my church. It makes me sad to say that they would believe it, but then they would say that the past is the past, and you're a new creature in Christ, and all that. I guess we're just learning a lot about it, and I hope we learn more, because for me at least, throughout therapy, my past has still been my present. When you go to sleep at night, and you're still having nightmares of what happened twenty years ago, it's hard to just say, "Well, my past is my past"; and, "I'm a new creature in Christ, and it's okay." It's not okay! The pain is still very much there and it's very much a part of your life.

But I am receiving healing, and it is coming through God. It's coming through my therapy, through people believing me and affirming me, from finding out that there have been other victims, that it's not just me, from people making me feel safe and accepted and not condemned.

Just one more thing right now. I want to answer the question, "How can I help you?" What did not help me was being quoted a Scripture, or being told to "buck up"; or, "God helps you"; or, "Can't you understand this?"; or, "Can't you see that?" I felt a lot of condemnation and a lot of misunderstanding, and that brought hopelessness to me. I feel fortunate that I've had a lot of help from a whole lot of people. The thing that helped most was that with each group of memories that came up, the new part of me, the new alter, was accepted and believed. A safe place was found for her, and she found out she was innocent. Even though the abusers told me it was my fault, we learned it wasn't.

Another thing that helped was the cleansing that God has given me! On Easter Sunday I got baptized again, and it was my third time! I'm just a baptism addict!

But it was just something God put on my heart; He led me to do it. There had been so much death put on me in the cult. They try to do the opposite of everything God wants to do for you. He wants to give us life, and they try to condemn you, even with the stuff they do in the cult. One thing they did was the slaughtering of babies.

One night they wrapped the skins of the babies they had slain, around me—around my naked body—and sent me into a corner, and said, "You will have to live with this." That was just a small part of a whole evening, if you can imagine. I mean, they go on and on!

But God showed me that baptism would symbolize that He had washed all that death off me—it wasn't there any more. I really didn't know what to expect. I told Jim I was going to do that. He encouraged me, and I went. I didn't tell my pastor about the satanic abuse; I just said to myself, "Lord, I was dedicated to the devil when I was a little girl, and that part of me wants to be dedicated to You now."

It was powerful! And I said to myself later, "If I ever get depressed again, I'm going to go swimming in that pool," because my baptism was so meaningful for me. I felt healed. My pastor, who didn't know anything about the satanic abuse, said, "Crystal, I want you to know that I feel like God's telling me something for you. You know, when God was bringing the children of Israel out of Egypt, they just kept screaming to Pharaoh, 'Let us go! Let us go!' " He went on, "I know that's been the cry of your heart from the time you were a little girl, and God wants you to know that you're free, that you're out!" And that's exactly what it felt like for me.

So it's been a continual thing. That was a healing time and I felt like I was all integrated—all my little pieces had come together! It was really great.

But then an emotional, traumatic thing happened to me just a week later. We talked about how that sort of disengaged me, but now I feel like the enemy dropped a scud missile on me!

You know, when something is bombed, it discloses, it uncovers what's there, and God used that for my good. He's uncovered some more memories for me that I'm able to bring out to Him for even more healing. So it has been a continual process.

I don't want to sound too "goody-two-shoes" or too spiritual, like this is fun, and it's all great, and it's all okay. It's not. You grow up in hell, and then you relive it. The physical feelings come back. I've stood in the shower, night after night, taking scalding hot showers. To be raped and beaten, and have the things done to you that they do in the cult is bad enough, but then I would go home and go through the same things with my mother's husband, with his children, and with anybody else he wanted to bring in on it. I told Jim once, "You know, most little kids come home from school, change into their play clothes, and go out and play. I would come home, and I wouldn't know when I was going to be beaten and raped, or by whom, or for how long, or anything!"

I grew up that way, so there was never any place for me to feel safe. So I built a new safe place for me. When we do imagery work, I have this house that has a room that nobody else knows about, so when I'm in there, nobody can come get me. I'm safe there.

That's what God has given back to me—His safety and my innocence, cleansing me from all that other, and making me feel loved. Maybe some day I'll feel that way. That's it for now.

* * *

Many of the people in the audience had never heard an SRA survivor talk so openly. They were stunned. Even those of us who were familiar with cult material were stunned. We each had to look within our own souls, and consider what we had heard. Crystal had talked matter-of-factly, and even managed to be a little light-hearted about some of her experiences. I was amazed that she got through it so well.

I quietly said a little prayer of thanks, and prayed that Crystal's strength would continue. In about thirty seconds we were ready to hear from Newheart.

3

NEWHEART:
The Key
Is Love

Jim: Okay, Crystal. We will come back to you a little later for questions. Now let's ask Pearl to introduce her client.

Pearl: This is Newheart. It's kind of an unusual name but it illustrates what happened when she gave her heart to Jesus. She was hard and angry and tough, and she fought a lot, but the moment she realized she didn't like being hurt, and the moment she found there was someone who wanted to come in and love her and rescue her from all she had been through, she called on the name of Jesus. In all my years, I've never seen such a transformation—instant transformation from a hard-hearted person to one who was filled with joy and love! Spontaneously I said to her, "You can't be called 'Mean Cleo' anymore. It doesn't fit you because now you have a new heart."

Newheart has not finished treatment yet. Her personalities are not united, but she wants to tell you about the healing God is doing in her.

Newheart: I was known as one of the persecutor personalities, and Jim said earlier today, in his Multiple Personality Disorder Treatment workshop, that they can become strong helpers. When I first came on the scene, Pearl [her therapist] was sitting on top of me, holding me down, because I was trashing the house. I went through a destructive period. I wanted to rip things apart. That was my job: "Hurt me! Hurt me! I don't care."

27

Pearl kept telling me over and over, "No. You didn't like the abuse. No. You didn't like it! It was bad, and it hurt you."

One day I broke down. I started to cry, and I said, "Yeah. Yeah. I am hurt."

And then she mentioned this guy, Jesus. She said He could help me. I was desperate. I had never heard of Jesus. She led me in prayer, and I asked Him into my heart, and the minute I did, the instant I looked up, the world looked different. The room looked different. She looked different. I said, "I don't feel like hurting you—or anybody—anymore." It was incredible, and that's how I got the name "Newheart."

"Kara" was the host personality. She was the one who grew up not knowing about anything, any pain at all. She just went to school and had a happy life while all of us took the abuse. But I love my name, because it tells about all Jesus did for me. It's exactly who I am—a new person in Christ.

It is pretty hard to think, after hearing Crystal, because hearing somebody else's memories, you know . . . all the parts of me that related were listening and I forgot who I was. Now I'm Newheart!

Now, let's see. I wanted to talk about what has helped me the most—helped all of us the most. I am going to go for a pretty controversial subject, and that is, what we needed most. We needed a family, a new mom and dad, so we could grow up again in a healthy environment, where we would not be hurt. I believe Kara was the person who told Pearl, "I feel like I need to go somewhere and have a brand new family, to be able to start my life all over again."

We had been getting hurt since we were real, real little. I think the mother didn't ever even touch us. She was one of those abandoning mothers, so we weren't only being abused, we also were not being loved at all either. So it ended up that God put it in Pearl's heart to provide the family—she and her husband and their family.

She took us into her home, and all of the little ones have been remothered, and they found out that all daddies aren't bad. I know for a fact that I wouldn't be where I am today if I hadn't had her and her husband. God has given us everything we needed. Pearl is still doing her fulltime work as a therapist, and inviting a multiple to live with you is like inviting two hundred people to live with you! There was a period when all the little ones were afraid of nighttime—the nighttime is the worst. Pearl would be up all night and then go to her job, taking me along, and I'd stay in the spare office. We knew that Jesus gave her everything she needed—her strength kept coming! The more she gave, the more she had to give.

Ever since I found out who Jesus was . . . First of all, when I found out He was a man, I thought, *Oh, great!* But then I found out He wasn't your average man! I have ended up having an incredibly close, close relationship with the Lord. I begged Him to reveal Himself to me, and to speak to me, and to let me hear His voice. Otherwise I wouldn't survive. He has done that. I hear Him in my heart. He told me that He put me with Pearl, and that I was to take everything I could get from her! He told me she would trust Him, and He would carry us down this road. The babies—there were all kinds of babies—she held them and rocked them. She has given them bottles.

And Kara, when she was here, asked Pearl, "Well, whatever personalities you meet, would you please tell them about the Lord?" And she has shared the gospel with every personality she has met. Even the Satanist personalities have come around, not because she was quoting Scripture all over the place, but she just loved them. All she has done is loved us. She has shown us, by just giving of herself, who Jesus is. Like Rebecca [an alter]—she was hurt bad by the Satanists. Rebecca was a Satanist—she believed that evil was more powerful than good. She challenged Pearl. It took quite a while, but she found out that the power coming out of Pearl was a lot stronger than the power she had.

I just want to tell you that, to help somebody like me, or us, you would have to love us first. Let the love of Christ flow through you, and then your words and the Scriptures will have credibility. Because, love . . . I don't know . . . love has just done everything for us. I know there are times when it wouldn't be appropriate for a therapist to invite a client to live with her (or him). But you also have to listen to the Holy Spirit. If He leads you to such a decision, and you have the resources available, then Jesus will work it out. We have seen many miracles.

There is something else I think has had a big impact on me in therapy. It just happened recently, in fact. I didn't want to come to this conference because I didn't want to find out how broken I am. I didn't want to hear it, because I've been feeling like I just want to die. There's no good reason to live. The other night, about a week ago, I told Pearl, "I just gotta talk to you." Lately all the personalities have been coming out, and slowly, Jesus has been turning the lights on so I can see the whole perspective—everybody at once, all the pain together. I know it's not all of it yet, but it's quite a bit of it. It has overwhelmed me. I just said, "I don't want to live, knowing all this!" I think I was the most desperate I've ever been. We went to Pearl's office in the evening. I don't remember quite what happened, but there was a flooding of emotion, and all these painful memories came to the surface. I told her, flat out, "There's no reason I can live."

She started to cry and cry, as hard as I was crying, and she said, "You're right. You know, if I were God, I would take you home. You shouldn't have to live any more. You have been through enough."

I stopped; I looked at her, and I said, "You really understand."

Not that she was giving me permission to die, but she really knew the extent of the pain, and that there really is no reason for me to live, without Christ. A verse that I hold on to, and that I claim is:

> I have been crucified with Christ, and it is no longer I who live, but Christ lives in me. And this life which I now live in the flesh I live by faith in the Son of God, who loved me and delivered himself up for me (Galatians 2:20).

I have no good reason to live, but neither do I have permission to take my life, because this life doesn't belong to me. It belongs to the Lord. I can't take it.

Whenever I tell Pearl I want to die, she says, "Okay, die to yourself and let Christ live in you." You can't say no to that. That has kept us on the road. We're still making progress, and I have a feeling that Jesus is going to do mighty things, because she and

I are teaming up. We are going to help Jesus put broken people back together.

Pearl: I think you'd want to hear a few words from me, since I'm on this journey with Newheart. I just want to say that when Kara, the host personality, revealed to me that she needed a family, I said, "Okay, we will find you a family like that."

When I started thinking, I had no idea the family would be ours. It was the last thing on my mind—I was psychoanalytically trained! The notion of risking my professional reputation, you know . . . I would nearly break out in hives just thinking about it! It became very clear to me, though. When the Holy Spirit prompts us to do something to help another person, it is important that we are willing to do it. He has blessed me and rewarded me in ways I can't even describe to you. Just seeing His faithfulness in being the one that takes the burden . . . I knew so many times that Kara wanted to die, and I knew I had no power of my own to keep her alive. But being able to give that up to the Lord, and seeing His faithfulness to us has been a tremendous mark in my own journey with Him. I would encourage you to care more about what the Lord thinks of you than what anyone else might think of you, and receive the blessing for that.

4

WILLIE MARIE:
Dolls
and Bears
and Poetry

Willie Marie: My story is very different from Crystal and Newheart's. I come from the farmlands of East Kansas and from a Christian home, and the hallmark of our family was isolation. That was a greater issue than any other, including maternal incest.

My mother was a dear Victorian lady, with her hair pinned up, who made it to all the church meetings—and played with her little kids at home. I guess I fragmented rather early. Most of my fragmentation is emotional. Most of my memories are intact, but I do a lot of daily dissociating, which unhooks my memory— like, Where did I put the cup?—but my life memories are pretty much together.

Two things helped me a great deal. I began to write and journal, and then at some point a poet fragment surfaced, one who wrote each memory in poem form. The memories came up randomly, but when they were all out I was able to put them together pretty much consecutively. So I have a book of poems that is my life's story.

I actually wrote it in sections, dealing with some molestation issues first, and then isolation issues. I began to piece it together, and then I added some poems that were vignettes of dysfunctional family living. Some were just hysterically funny! I threw them all together into this fat book [she held it up; it was about two inches thick], which is entitled, *Two Eyes*. It's my autobiography. This helped me with dissociation because before I wrote, I would remember something, and later I would remember something else, but I wouldn't remember them side by side. When I got them all on paper, I started reading, and I soon began to see that this family was tweaked! *Two Eyes* is a pun; it stands for *I*solation and *I*ncest.

Later I had another fragment surface, whom I named Gepetta, the toymaker. Both the poet and the toymaker have been my major decontaminator parts. They decontaminate the others before they fuse. These dolls [she swept her hand, pointing to about thirty dolls of many sizes, each more beautifully detailed than the last] are some of the toymaker's work. They look like fun creatures, which they are—I enjoy them immensely. But all kinds of emotional issues come out in the doll making.

I'm kissing off my childbearing years without ever having given birth—that is one of the issues the dolls help me with—that's why they are so baby-like. The little guy standing there represents my husband's baby, that I never got to have. He's blond and freckled, but we adopted a little boy who's brown-eyed and dark-haired. He is beautiful and a lot of fun, but not the baby I had imagined having with my husband when we married. When I made this doll, my son did not like him! [Laughs in the audience.] He picked up on enough of the emotional flavor of what I was working through as I made it to resent it.

I started two years ago with the dolls. A child alter surfaced, and she made it clear she wanted anatomically correct dolls. I had no idea what was coming down the pike! I just knew I was supposed to get those dolls.

When the first one came, I immediately took it into the house and wondered what would happen if I gave it water. From there I started making the cloth dolls. They're anatomically complete. They drink, they wet, they cry. They don't get their skin wet, even though they are made out of cloth.

My husband had some wonderful ideas about doll-making. The fingers are movable. Some of his technical expertise helped me, but when I got into the doll thing, more things surfaced, and I was able to put together what it was I was working through.

My mother did a lot of things that were just strange—it wasn't horribly abusive like the ritual stuff; it was just weird! She made us drink a pint of water every night when we went to bed. She dragged us out of bed at midnight, dumped another pint into us, and dumped another pint in us when we got up in the morning! So, all day long and all night long, we'd drink and go to the bathroom, drink and go to the bathroom.

Another weird thing surfaced. I brought home a doll I had purchased—it was a drink and wet doll—and after I got it home I gave it an enema. I put the water in the wrong end. I told Jim about it the next session, and he laughed. The next week the memories floated up—family enema time! I remember my parents stretching us out on the floor, the two of us, and giving us both enemas, side by side, myself and my brother. And I knew that was weird! A lot of things have come out with the dolls.

Another thing I express in my poems is my cynicism toward motherhood and parenting. This one is entitled, "Get a Doll." The personality fragment that contributed to this is Cinique—she's my cynic.

Cynique

I may not be understood,
    but to many contemplating motherhood
        my advice is:
            "Get a doll!"

It won't get sick
    or make a mess.
It will not vomit on your dress.
It won't defy you to your face.
It will bring you no disgrace.
It will not bring you shame
    by calling you some ugly name
        or screaming in a public place.

You will not warp its little soul
    with overmuch control.
If you neglect your doll,
    no harm is done.
You won't get a call

from some agency.
She is just for having fun
    when you want to play.

She's adorable and cute
    and she will stay that way.
She won't get mean
    or grow into a sassy teen
        with nasty things to say.

A doll won't fight.
A doll won't squall
    throughout the night.
She's Sugar and Spice
    without the price
        of doctor, dentist, shrink.
She won't drive you to the brink
    of insanity.

So, listen to me.
Take my advice:
    "Go, scrap it all
        and get a doll!"

(Quoted with the author's permission.)

[Laughter and applause.]

Jim: Do you want to say a few things about some of these dolls?

Willie Marie: There's Charity [the largest one on the table by far]. She's "the greatest of these!" [Lots of laughter.]

Jim: Why don't you hold her up, so we can see better how big she is.

Willie Marie: [Holding her up, so she stands by herself. She is about four and a half feet tall, and the audience makes noises of surprise.] She has bones and joints—elbows and knees, which my husband had to help me create.

Jim: Do you want to talk about the issues for each of these?

Willie Marie: The issue with Charity was my *standing up* to my husband's family, which was also dysfunctional, and ceasing to take abuse in that relationship. This is Joy. I don't know if Joy has any issue, other than to express the joy of life. She is made to crawl. That's why her head goes up. She praises the Lord when she sits up. This is Andrew. This one is Corky—this one walks. He was made to represent my husband—he's probably my favorite. He's one of the drink-and-wet babies. [His pants get wet when he is stood up, and everyone laughs.] My husband said, when I made this one, "You have to make him circumcised!" [Loud, sustained laughter!] So he's the only one who's circumcised. Never again!

All of them, from the least to the greatest are anatomically correct. This is my smallest drink-and-wet baby. This one is pre-born. [She opens a plastic egg.]

Jim: What was your issue prenatally?

Willie Marie: I don't know! I just liked a baby. Maybe it's pro-life!

And this is Molly, and Angelica. This is Squirt, but my friend calls him Wigglet. He has his own potty chair. [She places him on it, after undressing him properly, but his anatomically correct part spouts a nice little stream just before he reaches the chair. Another round of laughter is heard.]

Jim: He is supposed to go potty *in* the chair!

Willie Marie: Oh, well! You know how babies are!

Jim: Well, Willie Marie, why are these dolls for sale, if they are so cute and lovable?

Willie Marie: I don't know. [She pauses to think about the question. I later learned that a child fragment was out, who could think of no reason in the world to sell them!]

A friend of Willie Marie's from the audience: If these dolls can help someone else, because of the things that Willie Marie has worked through with them, then God bless them, and more power to them.

Willie Marie: [She was now a little more self-assured. An adult fragment had resurfaced.] Yes, I think they would be good dolls for the office, especially if you're a therapist working with children who've been sexually abused. I really wasn't able to touch my younger memories without them, because the language of a child is play. When my youngest parts came out, this was the only way they had to tell me, and other parts of my system, what they had been through, because they really weren't able to talk about it.

Jim: They would tell Gepetta about it, and she would make the doll before Willie even knew what she was making.

Willie Marie: Right. Gepetta would make the doll to accommodate the issue before I would know what the issue was. Gepetta is one of my more fun fragments. Another issue for the dolls is isolation—that's all I had as a child. I spent more time with dolls than with all the other people in the world put together! They became people to me, so I related to them. When my very young child parts are out, they are very comforted by the dolls. I had one young fragment out on the surface for quite some time; her name was Islette. People could go fly a kite if she could have only a dolly and a bear. That's all she wanted. I think she's a little more socialized now, but for a time, that was enough.

* * *

Willie Marie went back up to the platform, and sat in her chair, in front of her microphone.

Jim: [To the audience] I would say this is a good chance for you to wonder, out loud, what therapy is like for these people. We have two things going on here—we've got how creative play can propel therapy along; also, we have seen how the power of God has come to these people in different ways. If you have some questions you want to ask now, I think those areas would be fruitful for you.

* * *

Before we go to the "Questions and Answers" chapter, however, Willie Marie has kindly allowed me to include in this book a small part of her poetry collection. These poems, which disclose the process of her healing, are in the next chapter.

5

WILLIE MARIE:
Poems
Tell the Story

PEOPLE NEED to seek the most effective way of healing for their hurts. For dissociators, that often involves hooking memories up with the feelings that each event generated, and allowing the postponed healing to occur. Lacking that process, the feelings likely will keep pestering the person for no apparent reason.

Willie Marie found that composing poetry helped her in two ways: It prepared her to receive healing for the emerging memories; and it assisted the integrative process by allowing each of her parts to read the others' stories.

During the time Willie Marie was in therapy, many events emerged from her memory banks. She identified the parts of her which had held the experiences and the feelings, and the feelings were welcomed. Even disrupting, disgusting feelings. Healing came. The reader of these poems will be drawn into the tragedy and the triumph. May God be praised.

Pun

Throughout my childhood
there were
two unwholesome eyes
always watching me.

They were:

Isolation, and

Incest.

Isolation

You isolated us
out on the farm

alone.

You isolated me
within the home
upstairs
in the farthest room.

You thought to keep us "pure"
to insure
we would not be corrupted
by the wickedness
of the city.

What a pity
you ignored the sin
within.

(Matthew 15:19,20)

Inner Isolation

The Lonely Child
  became isolated
    from friends,
      family ...
        eventually
          from the rest of me;
            a sad and forlorn fragment
              of my personality.

Peekaboo

"Don't peek, now!" Mom says to brother
  as he sits behind the stove.
Then she takes me to the corner
  and pulls off all my clothes
    for the bath.
Across her lap,
  I'm on my back;
    my head hangs down.
"Spraddle out your legs," she says.
  I am exposed.
    The washing hurts.

He always peeks. She knows.

I feel naked,
  bare,
    on display for him to see;
    stripped of privacy,
      dignity,
      value.
Modesty is just a name.
Modesty is Mother's game
    of peekaboo
      with my body.

It's hard to take a day
  in May
    to honor Mother,
When it was Mom who set me up
  for incest
    with my brother.

Dissociation

The little girl this happens to
is not the same child that you
see at play.
Since the ritual is the same each day,
she can dissociate
so she won't hate
her mother.
She does not relate
her soreness with its cause.
She does not think of it
or let it come to mind
any other time.

Sex Education

My brother
told my mother
that the boy up on the hill
took the pants off
little neighbor Jill.

Mother said,
"Too bad.
Poor boy.
It's sad
he has no sisters.
He's had no way to learn
how girls are made."

Thanks, Mother!
You've added meaning
to my existence.
I'm an object lesson for this mass
you call my brother—
a demo model
for your sex education class.

Private Hell

It's an ugly dawn.
I feel disturbed.
I've been bothered.
He came in my room last night.
I've been touched without consent.
I don't know how I know,
    but I know.
I am perturbed:
    How far has he gone?
    How much has he done?
    How much has he seen?
    I cannot tell.
    I slept through everything.
    I am thirteen.
Fear,
    ignorance,
        superstition prevail.
This is private hell.

The Door

The white casing round my door
　　　is marred,
　　　scarred
　　　by the brown paint of my table.
Every night I hook my door
　　　and tie the hook down with a cord
　　　after the door is barred.
Then I barricade
　　　with table and chair.
I add pie pans to make noise
　　　in case the door is opened.
Still, some nights I waken screaming.
I am not dreaming.
My heart stops beating.
Then it pounds so slow, so hard,
　　　my chest feels like it will break open.
I know he comes in through the door.
He touches in my sleep.
　　　I sleep too deep.
　　　I do not waken.
At night he goes exploring.
By day he taunts me with a description
　　　of my hymen.
　　　He torments me
　　　　　relentlessly.
I am terrified.
What if it breaks?
What if he rapes me?
What if I keep on sleeping?

Mama says a girl who's not a virgin
　　　does not deserve to marry in white.
God protect me through the night.

Denial

My brother told me what he did.
One day
        on my mother's bed
                I told her what he said.
It took all my courage.
She said,
        "I don't think that's possible."

I felt so bad,
        dirty,
                crushed,
                        and sad.
I had never, never lied to her.
Why didn't she
        believe me?

Dear Abby

I wrote to Dear Abby
        and waited
                and waited
                        and waited.
Her letter came.
It said,
        "Your brother's actions toward you are not normal
        and should be stopped immediately
        before it's too late.
        If your mother will not listen to you,
        tell your father, and fast."

I knew what fast meant.
It meant you do not eat.
                You pray.
That day
        I prayed.
                I missed my supper.
That evening
        I told my father in the barn.

The Bar

My father
    glared at my brother
        without speaking.
Then he hammered on my door
    a two-by-four
        to which he screwed a bar.
His workmanship was poor.
He never painted it.
It was a scar,
    an ugly sore.
The old house was creaking.
Soon the bar no longer fit.

Three times I had asked for help.
I did not have strength to ask again.
I began my nightly barricade.

Hinges

My brother was huffed
    about the bar.
Privately
    he threatened me.
"I can still come in " he puffed.
"I can go out my window,
    sneak across the porch roof,
        and come in yours;
            or I can pull the hinges
                off your door."
He was bluffing but I didn't know.

The hinges were on his side.

Wholesome Perspective

All male calves
    were castrated into steers
        to sell for beef.
The family dog was neutered
    so he would not stray.
Male chickens fared worse:
    They wound up in frying pans
        while hens
            were kept for eggs.
It was plain to me.
Why didn't people see?
    Life's problems would be solved
        if we could just "fix" men!

I smile when people carry on
    about how wholesome life is on a farm!

Fantasy

"You're daydreaming again.
Pay attention!" my teacher complained.
My mind was not in class.
It had gone to some other time and place
    where I did not have to face
                fear.
I was a princess with beauty and grace,
    surrounded with maidens
        and children
            and ladies-in-waiting,
                and guarded by
                    ... eunuchs!
I slept safely in a vault.
My castle was securely barred.
No one ever made it past the guard.
They would halt
    all who came, except, of course,
        one faithful Prince on his white horse!

Broken Trust

Years had passed.
It was spring.
I was sixteen.
My friend was coming over.
My brother was ashamed.
He said,
>"Please have Dad take this awful bar
>>and two-by-four
>>>off your door.
>I promise:
>>I won't come in your room
>>>anymore."
He was getting tall.
He'd go to college in the fall.
I thought,
>"Why not?"
>(He was in tears.
>How could I not believe him?)

One more time
>he stole in.
I never trusted him
>again.

Atonement

My brother brought his college roommate
>home to me.
His roommate was respectful,
>friendly,
>>caring,
>>>gentle,
>>>>comfortable,
>>>>>safe . . .
>>>>>>and cute!
My brother knew I would accept his gift.
He said he did it to atone.
I married his roommate.
The debt was paid in full!

Prince

My Prince did come for me.
He was short and fair,
with freckles, golden hair.
He took me to a home beside the sea.
He was driving a black Ford Falcon
instead of riding a white steed,
but the man who came for me
was a Prince indeed!

Biddy

You Hag,
You old Bag!
You Biddy!
I miss you,
You Gritch!

Why
did you die?

When I came home,
You sang off key,
You cooked boiled beef for me,
You talked incessantly.

You Hag,
You Bag!
You Biddy!
I miss you,
You Gritch!

Why
did you die?
Why did you go?
Didn't you know
I would cry?

I loved you,
You Witch.

One Mother

Can a daughter
    divorce her mother,
        adopt another?
Maybe.

I have just one.
She is not divine.
But in spite of what she's done,
she is mine.
She is gone.
I cannot call her back,
    make her retrace
        her steps,
            force her to face
                what she chose to erase
                    from her mind.
Yet
I can choose to release
the debt.
There I find
        peace
of mind.

Henniger Flats

One day Jesus sent me on a solitary hike
to the top of the mountain.
He met me part way up,
and had me
list each memory.
When I reached the top,
one by one,
He took each ugly picture down
from the walls of my mind.
Behind
each space,
in its place
He made a door.
When I walked through, one by one,
He came into each moving scene.

When Mama turned me upside down for washing
He held up my head!
In the calf shed
Jesus arrived first when I screamed
and helped me get my clothing on.
Many times He wrapped me in His robe
and protected me
from touch
or view.
He respected me.
Nothing was the same.
Everything was new.
He took away the shame.
He restored my soul,
repaired my dignity.

He
cherished me!

Welcome Home
(Integration)

One day when Lonely Child appeared,
   I grabbed her and held on.
"You little snit,
   You split
      of me. You may not run.
         You must come home."

She tried
   to break away.
"This time you must stay
   and have your say."
She demanded that I guarantee
   protection
      and affection.
When she was satisfied
   that she was safe,
      she cried.
She stayed for many days,
   and she found ways
      to let the hurt come out.
Then she handed me back her soaked tissue.
She had faced her issue:
   She had been too vulnerable,
      too fragile,
         too loyal,
            to handle betrayal.

The person I have become
   turned to the child that I had been
      and said, "Welcome home, Lonely Child!
      Come in!
         You'll never be alone again!"
Then she curled up in my lap
   and took a nap.
At last,
   she integrated with my cast!

Unity

God grant me a single eye.   *(Matthew 6:22)*
   I confess,
      O Lord,
         my doublemindedness.   *(James 1:8)*
Unite my heart to fear your Name.   *(Psalm 86:11)*
Take my broken spirit, Lord,
   as a sacrifice.
O God, You will not despise
   my broken heart.   *(Psalm 51:17)*
I am shattered into parts,
   but You specialize
      in healing broken hearts!   *(Psalm 147:3)*

Eyes of God

The two unwholesome eyes
had limitations on their scope.
They could not hope
to overcome
the seven wholesome
eyes of God above
which watched me everywhere
with
Impeccable care.
Immeasurable wisdom.
Intimate healing.
Immense tenderness.
Intricate guidance.
Immaculate knowledge.
Infinite love.

6

QUESTIONS
AND ANSWERS

THE LISTENERS SENSED that, even though the things already shared had led to no outward display of emotions, the presenters' feelings must be very close to the surface. They had put themselves in a position of great vulnerability, and the audience respected that. Calmness and a deliberate pacing governed the questioning. After a short pause, a hand was raised and acknowledged.

Questioner #1: I'd like to address this to all three of you. In terms of how you dealt with your friends who knew you before you understood you were multiples, I'd like to ask whether or not they remained your friends, and what problems may have resulted by your going through therapy. I know I'm asking a big question, but how did you cope with those problems?

Crystal: I have had a change of friends. If I felt condemned by my friends, or that they didn't understand, or that they were minimizing my feelings or my situation, it was a big issue for me. Sometimes people would look at me, and say, "Oh, poor you; poor you." I don't want pity; I just want somebody to support me and believe me. I guess the most important thing is for them to confirm the fact that it wasn't my fault—it wasn't my choice. I'm still really careful. I'm guarded about the people I share with. I've been in my church two years, and I think I've shared with four people. It takes me a long time, and I'm very careful to make sure I know what kind of people they are before I share. Otherwise I'll feel totally abused again. It has happened, and still does, and it sets me back. So I am careful.

It's been hard, but sometimes support comes as a surprise. One of my childhood friends called me out of the blue recently. We haven't seen each other for about twenty years, and we began talking—catching up. When she covered the issues she had, I began to think, *That neighborhood should be wiped off the face of the earth.* It was astonishing the things that went on there. Then she began asking me questions, and I ended up telling her what happened with me. She was very supportive.

The members of my family were supportive, too, when they found out. I finally came to them and said, "Look. No more! You're not going to do this to me any more. I paid the price for all you guys!" I told them the truth, and you know it was really healing for me to have them know the truth. It made a lot of sense. It put everything in place, and I'm not the "black sheep" any more. But it's still hard. I guess, to answer your question, for me, it's still hard to find friends I feel safe with.

Jim: Just to clarify: In her case the family members were not the ones giving her the abuse. Maybe they were not helping much, but they were not the perpetrators. What Crystal did get from them was a lot of minimization, and that felt like more abuse. So she told them, "Don't minimize me! I've been through hell."

When she told them how bad it really was, they said, "We can believe that." That was lucky for her. It doesn't always happen that way. Too often, family members say, "Oh, yeah? Who believes that?" I am convinced that God prepared the hearts of her family so her story could come through to them in the way it should—and it was accepted. Any more comments about friends, and friendships?

Newheart: For me, Kara was the one who had all the friends as she grew up. She got married, and then was in a young marrieds' class at the church. She was "Miss Social"; she knew everybody. When I came on the scene I didn't know anybody because I was only out for abuse. For a time, Kara and I kind of competed, and I said to Pearl, "Kara's got all the friends. I want my own friends!" I wouldn't pick her friends!

During the past year, since Kara sort of left the scene, or we joined, and I'm the one with the body, I have Kara's memory now and I recognize people. I decided to go to church, and we let everybody know that I'm Newheart. I'm not Kara, but I have made friends with all of Kara's friends—well, not all of them. Some of them I don't like. [Laughter.]

People who have Jesus in their heart and who are willing to stretch themselves have accepted me for who I am. Most of them who knew Kara, and know me, say they notice the difference, and they like me much better! [More laughter.]

Pearl: You want to tell them why?

Newheart: Because I'm much deeper.

Pearl: She doesn't have to pretend everything's fine, and that's very attractive, isn't it?

Willie Marie: I don't know if I've had to face what you're talking about. Circumstances have moved many of my close friends away, again bringing on the isolation issue with me. But the Lord has blessed me with three friends who are fragmented also, and that is very nice. I'm not in contact with one of them right now, but I still have the two others, and that's good. It takes very little for me to feel isolated. Whenever a friend moves away, I face isolation again.

Newheart: I have had quite a few experiences with Kara's friends from the past who think it's a little too weird, and they haven't wanted to do things with me. That has been just fine—it hasn't undone me. I think it's not in their capacity to understand, or they don't want to, so that's all right.

Questioner #2: I am different from most of you here. I'm a pastor and not a clinical psychologist or a counselor, but I do a lot of counseling. I want to ask a practical question to all of you. There are a number of ladies in my church, and they, unlike everybody else, don't hear the same thing. When we share the Scriptures, or we share about the love of the Lord, or anything like that, I can tell they hear it through different ears. Can you give me advice, as to how, as a pastor, I can minister to them? [Silence] Could you hear my question?

Crystal: How we heard it is the question! [Lots of laughter and applause!]

Questioner #2: I'll go a little further to say I've heard a lot of what you're talking about before, but all of a sudden now, it's clicking. I've heard some of what these women have experienced in the past, and my guess is that they don't really know what they're dealing with. Crystal, you mentioned it once. You said when people share Scriptures with you to try to encourage you, it doesn't. But the love . . . a lot of that comes through. When we discuss anything in the whole area of the Father's love, the character of God, His identity, things like that, I hear these backgrounds. A common thing these women say is, "You don't understand what I've been through," and I have to reply, "You're right. I don't understand."

Crystal: That's the best thing you can say.

Questioner #2: What do you look for in a support group in your church?

Crystal: I don't want to condemn the church—I was very much involved in it, very much a part. I was being ministered to, and people did everything they could to help me for ten years. Then the depression got so bad that I just said, "I can't do this any more," and I went into therapy. So a lot of healing was given to me.

I guess it was sort of like pulling the weeds outside the house, and when I got into therapy, we went *into the house!* And it was a mess!

Like I said before, when something hurts these women, if they knew they could come to you and tell you what it meant to them and why it hurt, and ask you what you meant when you said it, you could work it out together.

With me, a lot of the time, people would say, "You need to forgive them"; or, "You need to forgive yourself." Now that means to me that I did something wrong—I did something that needed forgiving! The cult used to use guilt and blame to control me. They made me believe I had chosen to join them, but that was not true. So if I didn't do anything wrong (this is what I am working on now in therapy), why am I being blamed at church? If I didn't do anything wrong, I shouldn't get all that blame from church people.

There are other things. Just this last Sunday in church, they were talking about Josiah, the one who was king when he was just 8 years old, and this is how different things affect different people. The pastor talked about how Josiah had a horrible family, and how he watched his father be slaughtered by the people who hated him so much because of how horrible he was.

Yet at the age of 8, he was the king of this nation. Then the pastor said, "You would think that after being through all that he would need years of therapy to get a grip on his life."

I understood what the pastor was saying. But to me, that meant *Okay, I'm in therapy because I don't have a grip on my life.* I started feeling condemned and actually sat there in tears! And that really wasn't what he meant, but the cult people put so much condemnation on you, and so much blame, that anytime somebody gets near me like that, it's like you're coming at me with fire, and I was burned in one! What seems to help me most is I usually go into Jim's office on Thursday, and cry, "AAAAAAH!" I'm able to talk it out, and find out what the truth is for me. I'm getting so much better at just being able to say, "Well, maybe they don't understand, or maybe they do, and maybe that was great for Josiah—he didn't have to go into therapy." I guess I'm starting to not take everything my pastor says as though it's a sermon directed toward Crystal. I realize he's making another point, and knowing that, I know he's not out to get me.

It might help if you were to stand up and say that. Tell your people, "If I say something that hurts you, come tell me." It really is healing to know you don't have to be the victim any more, and, if something hurts, you can do something about it.

Questioner #3: I am interested in what kinds of characteristics and qualities in therapists you three have found most helpful.

Willie: It is important to be believed. It's important to be affirmed. And for me, it was important that he was free-wheeling enough to read half a dozen poems every week, and feed my drink-and-wet dolls, and change their diapers with me when I had a small personality fragment out! Whatever facilitated my healing was okay.

Newheart: I would say, first of all, being believed. When the stuff comes out of my mouth, I'll say it and then take it back with, "No, that didn't happen." It's true, but I still try to say it isn't a lot of times. It's been so helpful for me that Pearl lets me know she is convinced that all of this is true. Whenever I deny it, she's able to bring me back around to seeing the truth. Also just . . . I would just call it love . . . the love of the Lord. She lets Jesus' love flow through her.

When the alters come out, she is willing to do whatever they need. Kiddy, a 3-year-old alter, was always hurting in her stomach because of the dad's abuse. When she first came out, Pearl took her out in her car, during a break, and bought her a pink blanket and some Pepto Bismol. Even though it was psychosomatic pain, Pearl treated it like Kiddy was really hurting. Pearl basically just loved us. Just love! It's very easy for a person with Jesus in their heart to do that!

Crystal: Somebody asked me this morning if I was a therapist, and I laughed. I said, "No, I'm his patient." [Turning to face Jim, she continued.] Now you're going to get embarrassed! [Loud laughter.] He has been a real gift from God to me in a lot of ways. Because my faith is so important to me, he's functioned as both a pastor and a therapist. I don't know how he does that, but he does.

I guess we are all saying how important it is to be believed. He was the first one who allowed me to just be angry and ornery, and when I said bad words he didn't flinch. I was allowed to express all my emotions—and they don't come out pretty at all. When they've been stuck down there, it's like throwing up! It's got to come up to come out. It's ugly, and it's awful, and I never before felt the freedom to be that way—but I could in therapy. Other people who sometimes are in sessions with me—in fact I've got another appointment with a woman therapist—just believe me, and they never take the opposite side, which some had done in previous counseling sessions. They seemed to say, "Okay, let's find out what's wrong with Crystal, and then we'll solve that problem." Jim and my lady therapist wanted to hear me—to listen to me and to believe me—and to find out what had been done wrong *to* me. And that made a big difference to me.

We would find the source of the pain, and then I was able to get healing. I was not able to get that before.

Questioner #4: I just want to acknowledge how grateful I am for your courage to share. What a tremendous benefit it is to me and my clients! I have two questions: One is, How have you processed the question about God's image—about how a loving God can allow such abuse to happen? The second is, What do you do with rage, and with the whole matter of forgiveness?

Crystal: Those are big issues for me. I don't force anything on myself anymore, and it doesn't happen in therapy either. If I don't see a loving God, I don't get condemned with, "Well, that's what the Bible says." God has been really faithful and patient with me.

Just one little story. A couple of weeks ago we were in a session because I had been having a lot of memories coming up from a different place. It was of ritual abuse, but it was at a place different from the other memories. It was a different bank of memories for me; my friend was in therapy with me, and Jim was there, too.

Sometimes when I first start remembering I'll talk about it as though I'm reading a book about somebody else. Then if I'm in a safe place, I can hook up with the feelings and can deal with them. I walk out feeling like I've been to the doctor and dealt with the problem, instead of just getting harmed—just getting split open.

Anyway, they had been talking to me—it had been a hard session. Jim stopped, and he said, "You know, when I was talking about such and such . . . " and I looked up at him and said, "No, I don't."

Then he said, "Hum. Remember when I said such and such," and he kept going.

And I said, "I don't remember a thing you said."

So we realized I had blocked out a lot from the therapy session. The reason I bring this up is to share that, when we went into those memories, it dealt with the part of me that was terrorized the most by my mother's third husband.

He was in charge the night of those memories. He got to do whatever he wanted to coerce me into staying in the cult. My mother was divorcing him, and so they wouldn't have access to me anymore. That was my worst night, and when we went back to talk about those memories, I said, "That's the part of me that used to stay hidden in my closet."

I would go into my closet in my room, and I would hide there, behind my stuffed animals, hoping he wouldn't find me. But he would come and do whatever he wanted in my closet, using my stuffed animals to smother me to keep me quiet, or he would drag me out. So even my little closet wasn't a safe place for me, but that's where I was, where those memories, that hurt part of me, was.

So we talked about going into the closet. Now, one thing that's always hard for me is when someone says, "Does it help you to know that Jesus was with you there?"

And I look at them, and I think, *Are you cracked?* Because, no it doesn't. For some people that's healing, but it doesn't help me—it offends me.

So we talked about bringing healing to that little girl in the closet. And so my friend, Kay Kay, could come in because she's a survivor; I could trust her. She came in, and just held me in her arms. Jim got to be there because he's big and strong, and when I'm going through these he's on my side. He's there to protect me. He knows the bad guy and he believes me.

Then we talked about Jesus coming in, and I said, "I don't really know Him. I don't really trust Him." That part of me didn't. But then I said, "Okay. Okay, I'll let Him in."

So the picture I got at that time—and I believe it was God showing me His love for me, not just imagery work I was doing, but the Holy Spirit—Jesus came in and He picked me up in His arms, and He began wiping off all the muck and all the stuff they had made me live in that night—all the stuff they had forced me into, and shoved my face into. That was healing to me, and it started with me being able to say, "I don't know Him."

So, parts of me know God, but parts of me don't know Him, and being allowed to say that I don't understand Him, or I don't know why He let me go through all of that, is the beginning. It helps me be able to work through all the lies they put on me—telling me that Jesus didn't love me—and all the things they did to destroy my image of Him. I can reach the point where I find out He really does love me, and I am safe with Him, and I do have hope for the future.

Jim: How about rage? That was the second part.

Crystal: [To the therapists in the audience.] Well, when you guys find out how to deal with that, you just let me know! [Laughter and applause.]

Jim: Any of you want to talk about rage?

Newheart: Well, I have a lot of ragers inside. Thank God, Pearl is really strong and she can take me down, 'cause there's been a lot of wrestling, if that's what you want to call it. I guess that's another quality of a therapist—she's strong. When we want to express rage, we hit things and bang on walls. And every time I get hold of a stuffed animal I get pictures of that other mother, and I try to tear its arms or head off, or burn it. There are a lot of ways to express rage.

Pearl: I think it needs to be acknowledged. But if it gets to the point where property or people could be damaged, then intervention is necessary. At that point, the rage needs to be contained.

Willie Marie: One of my friends who is also fragmented gave me a good suggestion when I was going through some intense anger toward my father. She suggested getting some playdough, a butcher knife and a cutting board, and creating a facsimile of what it is you're angry at, and cutting it up. It was wonderful therapy for me. My husband came into the room one time, and there I was sitting in the middle of the bed, hacking this thing to smithereens. [Pause] He walked out. I told Jim about it the next session, and he said, "Smart man!" [Laughter.]

Jim: Rage is hard to get a grasp on if you are just trying to express it. Expressing it is not the goal, though that may be required, but healing is the goal. The way I approach rage is to expect that there is always hurt underneath, and rage spins off from that. To find healing for the hurt—the pain from the abuse that happened so long ago—will reduce the rage. To search for the painful memories that prompted the rage in the first place, is my approach.

Questioner #5: I too have been touched by your courage. A lot of times our history becomes something that God uses to empower us, and I sense He has done that for you. My question is, Have you given any thought to how God might use you in the future, about what you might do with your story or history in a way that only you, who are gifted in the ability to reach out to us in an empowering way, can? Have you given any thought to what you might do?

Newheart: I'm glad you asked that. I've given it a lot of thought, and so has Pearl, and our family.

I feel that I've gone through my process much faster because God has been in it. I believe I know what people like me need; they especially need Jesus. I don't see how anybody can have a broken brain and get it fixed without Jesus. You just can't do it without it being a miracle from Him.

Our dream is to have a place, a home for multiples. It'll be called "Change of Heart." People like us don't necessarily need to be hospitalized, because we're not crazy, but we do have a great deal of pain and a lot of stuff to work through. What we need is support and a safe place.

So I would like to see a place with room for up to ten multiples at a time. We could have group therapy, and the child alters could come out and do therapy together. They could have play therapy. Everybody would have a roommate, because the nighttime is awful. You could feel safe at night, and you'd have somebody to talk to. It's going to be an incredible place. We're waiting for Jesus to give us the money and resources and everything we need to make it happen. I'd also like to write a book.

Willie Marie: I guess I've written my book. I'm thinking about publishing it at this point. I really don't know. I feel like I've been very much on the shelf in many ways for the last three years. I'm not one of the "doo-zers" at church. I'm not on all the ladies' social committees. I may be taking a hike, making a doll or writing a poem. I've had a lot of good healthy time to myself, which is the up side of isolation. I have a lot of parts who know how to be alone, and how to make creative use of alone time. So, I don't know what I'll get into, so far as getting back into the church mainstream in ministering. I really don't know.

Crystal: I guess the part of the healing God has brought to me since I've been in therapy is that He doesn't want to just use me. I received the Lord when I was 21, and during the ten years before I started therapy I was strong in my church and in ministry. But at the end of that time, I still had all this pain that had not been ministered to. The emphasis was on ministry, and serving—"Get out there and forget about yourself, and you will be healed."

There was a lot of attention given to me at the same time, but I left feeling kind of used, that God didn't care about *me*, but just what I *did!* So there's been a process of redeeming that. God spoke to me clearly once and said, "I don't want to use you." It's not that He doesn't want to use me for good, but He doesn't want to use me in any abusive way—almost like He was saying, "I didn't make you just to do My farm work." He made me because He loves me, and cares about me.

It's out of my relationship with God, and out of the healing, that I do want to be used in a meaningful way. One Scripture that He strongly impressed on me, a long time ago when I was asking Him why, was that "with the same comfort you have received, you will comfort others."

The blessing of my life has been that God lets me give comfort to some of those who are in difficult situations. Most of the time they felt that other people didn't understand them, or they were embarrassed, or ashamed, or felt helpless. Just this last month, what's happened is that I get to take care of the babies in the church! And that's neat for me, because in the cult they harmed babies so unmercifully. Now, to be able to hold them and protect them, and tell them I love them, and have them feel safe, is especially healing for me, and I love doing that.

Then this week I was told that I get to be on the prayer team at church. I was a little unsure about that, because the people who are on that team know about my background. They know I was ritualized and all that. I thought they might be a little nervous about having me on the prayer team, but I can still be getting healed. At the same time I can give out of my healing—I can give out of the parts that are whole. God has given me so much.

When people come up to me, the only thing I want to tell them is that God loves them and that He does understand them, and from then on it's like God simply takes over. It's more of a blessing for me to be a part of, rather than looking at, what I can do for others.

Questioner #6: I know of a multiple who has incredible gifts, and I'm wondering, when the integration has taken place, what will happen to all those gifts? Will she still have them?

Willie: If she's integrated properly, with bringing each broken piece to the Savior, she will still have the gifts. One book I read on multiplicity really disturbed me. The more I thought about it, the more I concluded that the presence with her that she called "Michael" had to be demonic. His way of helping her with integration, was to take her into some kind of spinning dance and spin off the alters. She came out of the experience with less than she'd had. She ended up with people who didn't know how to tie their shoes! This was a horrible thing. It's totally opposite to the way Jim has been helping me integrate, where you bring every part together. He describes it as layering transparencies over each other. As I placed the different layers of my house over each other, you could see through; they all came together and nothing was lost.

Jim: Just to add to that, it seems that when the dissociation is still working heavily, you'll have periods with lots of artwork, and lots of artwork, and lots of artwork, or poetry, or doll-making, and then nothing for a while—at least no expressing that points toward healing. So that seems to disappear. After the integration has been finished, things can be modulated—a little bit of artwork here and a little bit there—but the creativity certainly is not lost. It's just moderated—not so many ups and downs.

Questioner #7: Do you fear retribution from the cult?

Crystal: I used to. Part of my response to that is, "You've done everything you can do to me, so what have I got to lose?"

The worst they can do is kill me, and if they do, I will go home and be with Jesus. So much of the time here I'm in pain, so that's where I want to be anyway! Plus, I'm single and have no children.

But, yes, that is the biggest thing with uncovering each block of memories. The story always ended with them threatening me, telling me I could never get away from them; they would find me wherever I went. They did some hard work on me because I didn't want to be there—remember, I supposedly had a choice—my mother was divorcing this man. He was not my birth parent, and I never wanted to be there. I had nightmares about being demon possessed almost my whole life. I haven't had one for a long time, now.

As the memories come back, I'm able to realize that's where so many of the feelings come from. The fear has been immense. Jim finally suggested that I put a lock on my bedroom door, and do whatever other practical things I could to make myself feel safer. For the most part, you just don't know who to trust—whether a person is your friend or your enemy. That may be why I don't have a bigger support system at church. In the cult they tell you that your friends are your enemies, and when you're with your family and your friends, you can't tell them what's been done, because they've threatened your mother. They threaten that the police will come get you, and that you will be blamed for everything. It just goes on and on.

Questioner #7: Have there been any messages from the cult since you left?

Crystal: Have they contacted me? Not that I know of, but this is the first time I've spoken in public about it.

Questioner #8: Did any of you ever get involved in cutting yourself or injuring yourself?

Newheart: The desire has been there quite a lot. I believe one of the personalities tried, but she was caught. I've been through a number of deliverances, and the demons had made me want to walk through windows a lot! All those windows! There is a lot of push to cut, cut, cut. My hand did go through one window, but it was because a 5-year-old was hysterical, not because I tried to do it.

Questioner #8: Do you have any sense of their purpose—why the demons did that?

Pearl: To kill her, I think. Satan has come to steal and destroy, and to kill the temple where the Holy Spirit lives. We've taken the approach that no matter what the impulse is, especially before deliverance times, she has needed a bodyguard, someone to care for her because those times can be very destructive. We've had the bodyguards there, but the main point is that your body is the temple of God, and no matter what you feel like doing, you are not to hurt yourself. So, if she doesn't have the control to protect herself, we take additional measures to give her that control.

Jim: Just a comment about the cutting. It seems to be different from person to person. Sometimes its a relief to them—at least they know they are alive while they are cutting. One of them said, "I didn't even know I was alive a few minutes ago."

In other cases it's a persecutor alter, trying to end it all. They start with a little bit, and then a little bit more, and the alter will hope that the next time they can finish the body off. But they get resistance—they start cutting and then they stop because the other personalities start crying, "No! No! No!" So from personality system to system, there is no single way of looking at it.

Questioner #9: I appreciate, extremely, your courage in talking about the physical stuff—the wrestling and all. During deliverance, have you ever experienced demons coming out angry and coming at you, trying to kill you or the therapist during the process?

Jim: I think I can speak for Crystal and Willie. It's been effective to bind the spirits ahead of time, in the name of Jesus, and it's gone without incident.

Newheart: I've had the same experience. The people helping with the deliverance have known a lot, so they've been careful to not allow any demons the ability to manifest themselves. It's been calm and quiet. I think a couple of personalities she shared Christ with banged their heads like demons were making my body hit the wall and banging my head, but it was the Satanist personalities. No real damage.

Pearl: One time, the day before a deliverance, we knew there was a lot of tension within the system. We were sitting across the table from one another, and a strange look came over her face. She looked at the coffee cup I had in front of me. I said, "What was that thought?"

She said, "I was thinking about throwing this hot coffee on you."

One thing we noticed for sure. Generally there's a very positive, trusting, affectionate relationship, but the demonic influences hated me. So it was like a litmus test—whenever she withdrew, or whenever she had an angry look on her face, that was the result of the demonic influence. It was evident we needed to look into that.

Jim: We are about out of time. [To the panelists.] Any P.S.s? Any follow-ups? Any final thoughts?

Willie Marie: In my case, quite a few spirits were involved, more than I ever would have guessed when I started. I come from a Christian background, and they didn't really have a lot of power because of the choices I've made in my life. You can have spirits stuck there from birth, but they have very little power to mess with your life if you've never given them the reins with your choices. They'll stay, though, until you kick them out. They will influence you in subtle ways. There's a difference in the strength of the demon and the strength of its foothold. Some of mine had strong footholds because the abuse was hidden. It was well covered, and I wasn't aware of what was going on with me. But the spirits themselves had very little power to affect my behavior.

Pearl: I have a P.S. I think this is a big statement for the power of Jesus over the power of darkness, and I personally respect everybody here that's willing to make a stand. I think the more we are open about these things that are done to precious people, and about the way to get healing, the weaker the enemy will be.

Newheart: Like I said in the beginning, I didn't want to come to this seminar at all because I had attended one in San Francisco where they attempted to talk about the ritual abuse without getting into the spiritual aspect of it. The teacher tried to not talk about evil and good. That was appalling to me. You cannot address these things without talking about demons or spiritual warfare or evil. I left there feeling like I wasn't a person; I was an it. There were a lot of jokes that offended me greatly. Here I feel like I am a person and that everybody here is so supportive. I just say thank you, and . . . go get 'em, and let Jesus be your guide!

Crystal: There was something I wanted to share earlier. Now that I have a second chance, I will. I feel a little uncomfortable talking so much about God, and how He's helped me. I know you want to know what you can do from a therapeutic point of view, but you're all Christians, so I guess you're asking for that, too.

I don't want to minimize at all how hard it is to go through— like if you just put the right scriptural bandaid on it, or name the right demon, then it's okay. It's really a hard process. You have to undo something that was put up so strongly and so painfully. But there are a couple of Scriptures I've been reading this last week that have helped me a lot. I was really feeling down again, and crummy. So I keep reading them to my selves . . . and . . . can I read them here real quick?

Jim: Of course.

Crystal: These scriptures speak to me of what God's promising to do for me—what He has done, and also what He's promising to do for me for those parts of me that are feeling very painful right now. They are out of Isaiah. In chapter 54, verse 4, it starts:

> Fear not, for you will not be put to shame; neither feel humiliated, for you will not be disgraced; but you will forget the shame of your youth.

And then beginning with verse 11:

> O afflicted one, storm-tossed, and not comforted, behold, I will set your stones in antimony, and your foundations I will lay in sapphires. Moreover, I will make your battlements of rubies, and your gates of crystal, and your entire wall of precious stones. And all your sons will be taught of the LORD, and the well-being of your sons will be great. In righteousness you will be established; you will be far from oppression, for you will not fear; and from terror, for it will not come near you.

> If anyone fiercely assails you, it will not be from Me.
> Whoever assails you will fall because of you. Behold, I
> Myself have created the smith who blows the fire of coals,
> and brings out a weapon for its work; and I have created the
> destroyer to ruin. No weapon that is formed against you
> shall prosper; and every tongue that accuses you in judg-
> ment, you will condemn. This is the heritage of the servants
> of the LORD.

Just one other one:

> The Spirit of the LORD GOD is upon me, because the LORD
> has anointed me to bring good news to the afflicted; He has
> sent me to bind up the broken hearted, to proclaim liberty to
> captives, and freedom to prisoners; to proclaim the
> favorable year of the LORD, and the
> day of vengeance of our God; to comfort all those who
> mourn, to grant those who mourn in Zion, giving them a
> garland instead of ashes, the oil of gladness instead of
> mourning, the mantle of praise instead of the spirit of faint-
> ing. So they will be called oaks of righteousness,
> the planting of the LORD, that He may be glorified"
> (Isaiah 61:1-3).

And that's just what I think God is doing, through my therapy, for me.

Pearl: I think it would be appropriate to ask each of you, when you find Crystal, Willie, or Newheart coming to your mind, to pray for them. They are on the road—their trip isn't over. I think they would be very grateful to know that, as they are giving the gift of themselves to you, you will also remember them in prayer.

7

CRYSTAL: God's Mercy

MANY SURVIVORS are not in a position to confront their perpetrators. Most can hope for no mercy. The abuse happened, and that cannot be changed. The events will never be completely erased. But people can hope that the abusers will be identified in order to protect future victims.

If the abuse happened only once, that would be too often. If it happens at all, it usually happens often. If the impulse within the perpetrator is strong enough to abuse a child once, it is likely to be strong enough to abuse other children at other times. The abusers should be stopped, and people in the mental health profession work very hard to achieve that.

In practicality, solid evidence of abuse is hard to find. Child abusers want to hide their madness, because if it were exposed, their lives would be changed forever—public humiliation and jail, with a stigmatized reputation thereafter.

When the crime against children is as heinous as one can imagine, the evidence will be hidden as well as one can imagine. The more dastardly a crime is, the harder it is to believe. The most effective way to hide a crime may be to carry it out in as dastardly a way as possible, in the most repulsive, grotesque way imaginable. It is hard for judges and juries to believe that anybody would do certain things to children, especially the things reported by satanic ritual abuse survivors. People keep hoping it is not true. When the public accepts the fact that SRA really happens, the way our justice system operates will have to be changed. Changes are usually hard to implement, and changes in protecting the rights of the accused while also protecting survivors will certainly not be made easily. At present, the justice system is not set up to consider seriously how to deal with SRA. There are too many roadblocks to admissable evidence, and too little protection for witnesses.

Crystal has tried to make some progress in uncovering the crimes of her perpetrators. Here are parts of a letter she sent to the detective in charge of investigating her evidence:

Dear Detective Donald:

I don't know if you will recall my last conversation with you 11 months ago. I explained at that time that I had been unable to complete a report about Jerry Smythe because I was still battling severe depression, and the memories were still coming back too strongly. I've had to fight just to get through the day, and the thought of writing a report detailing these horrid events has been overwhelming to me. I've tried working on it bit by bit. I apologize for it taking me so long to get this to you. I know I will not be able to detail all the events that occurred over a seven-year period, but I hope it will be enough for you to begin an investigation. Many times I agonize over the fact that without doubt, Jerry Smythe is still beating, raping and torturing little boys and girls with each day that passes. That is what has forced me to write this.

The first incident occurred while I resided with my mother and stepfather. I was 6 years old, and as I was walking home one day, Jerry Smythe drove up beside me in his car and stopped with his car window down. I recognized him as the man who lived down the street. He instructed me to get into his car, that he was taking me to the doctor's. Since there were quite a few doctors living in our neighborhood, I believed him. I had been taught to respect doctors and obey authority. I got in the car and went along. I was taken to a location that was in a very "seedy" area. It was a rundown building with a secured entrance. We stood on the front steps after ringing the bell waiting for someone to let us in. A man with a white coat on appeared at the door. Although he was not clean and shaved, and was ragged looking, I still believed he was a doctor. I was introduced to this "doctor" and taken into the examining room where I was left alone with this man. The room had an examining table in it and a dresser against the wall which had a glass jar and what looked like doctor's instruments on it. One of the walls was glass with a sort of dark cloudy reflective glass or mirror in it. Mr. Smythe was in the room on the other side of this glass. The doctor told me to take my clothes off and to put on a small white gown he gave me. He didn't leave the room, he watched me undress, telling me to take my panties off. The doctor made comments as I undressed, saying things like, "Very nice. You're a very pretty little girl, you know. How would you like to be my special little patient?" He lifted me up onto the examining table and began his "examination."

Crystal described exactly the things he did to her, with all the details, from one moment to the next. He violated her in many ways. She was cleaned up and led out by Mr. Smythe, and while he was taking Crystal home, he told her it was his turn, and did those same things to her, too. Here is how he guaranteed her silence:

Mr. Smythe told me I could never tell anyone about this, that if I did, my stepfather and mother would send me away to a home for bad girls who lie. A place where I would never go out to play or see my family again. A place that was dark with no windows, where no one would ever find me so they wouldn't have to feel ashamed of me. I would never see my dog again, and men could come get me and do whatever they wanted with me and the other bad little girls. But if I didn't tell, then he would never tell anyone what I did that day. In complete fear and terror, I accepted this.

A few years later, Crystal's stepfather moved away, and her mother, an extreme alcoholic, had an affair with Mr. Smythe. This gave him frequent access to Crystal, any time of day. The terror was constant. There was not a safe place in the house, day or night. Her letter to the detective chronicled her life until Mr. Smythe moved out of the neighborhood. For ten pages, Crystal's details continued, with lots of specifics and names and dates. Smythe was involved in a cult which subjected Crystal to ritual abuse. The pages in which Crystal recounted satanic ritual abuse (SRA) were very graphic. Murder and terror and torture and perversion—crimes as heinous as one can imagine. She continued on page 10:

The only way I could cope with it was to completely block it out of my mind. I didn't want to be that little girl. So I made her go away. I have spent my life locked up in my own little private hell. I still do not sleep through the night. I still have nightmares. I still have a great deal of anxiety. And the worst of it all is the depression. It is like heavy chains that I have carried with me all my life. It has kept me imprisoned, and kept me from living the life that every human being was given. While my friends went on with their lives, to college, and families, it is often all I can do to get through the day. Sometimes, if I can just get out of bed, if I can just not kill myself today, then that's a far better feat for me than what most people would consider an accomplishment in their lives. There are many things I have longed to do and been unable, because all my strength and energy is taken up with just getting through. He stole my childhood from me. My life was and sometimes still is a living hell. Without end. I would rather have cancer than to battle this depression, or to deal with the memories of these events. There are many times I would rather be dead. It is my own silent private hell.

I pray to God that you are somehow able to keep this man from hurting others. From destroying other children's lives. As long as he is free, I have no doubt, no doubt at all, that he is continuing to do this. He will never stop as long as he is free.

I know, Detective Donald, that when Smythe finds out that I have told you about this, he will try to harm me, my animals, and/or my home. Whether it be himself, or more likely, someone else he will send, I believe he will do all he can to harm me, to harass and terrorize me. The only purpose I can find in surviving all this is in the hope of helping to keep others from suffering this way. He has done everything to me you can possibly do to a human being. He has violated my mind, my soul, my body. There's really nothing left for him to do to me. I pray to God that he is stopped—for the sake of others. Please don't let him hurt any other little children. Please.

Sincerely,
Crystal

Jim: So what has happened since you sent the letter?

Crystal: When I first made a telephone call to him, he was very supportive. He assured me that if I sent him a letter, he would take care of it, and that Smythe would be investigated. But when I mailed it I found out he had been transferred to another division. I tried to call there to see what the deal was, but it was like the letter was mailed off to Mars or somewhere. The detective couldn't even come to the phone. I was given the name of some other man. Finally, after a couple of weeks of calling, I was able to get through to Detective Donald, and I was told there was nothing they can do except put the letter in a file. They couldn't question anyone else in the neighborhood to find out if any of the other kids had been harmed by him, because that would be slandering him. So in essence, they protected him and didn't protect any of the other kids. That's the way the laws work, I guess. Any kid around him is in danger, and there's absolutely nothing I can do to stop it.

Jim: That is so depressing. What can you do? Are there legal alternatives?

Crystal: My whole purpose for sending that letter was for the sake of the other kids. There is nothing I can do to turn back the clock or make it go away. The letter was not a vengeful thing. After I realized that nothing was going to be done by the police, I considered the option of a lawsuit to bring to light the things Smythe had done. Maybe that would keep him from harming somebody else. I called the L. A. County Women Commission's Task Force on Ritual Abuse, and was given the name of an attorney. I was told by this man that it is an extremely hard thing to prove, and that it would cost thousands and thousands of dollars. I would have to come up with a huge retainer fee, pay him $250 an hour, and pay for the investigator. It would cost an enormous amount. I've worked so hard to make a life for myself, it sounded like I would have to give that all up if I wanted to sue him. I would have to work a long time just to pay for the lawsuit, to keep it going.

Jim: What did the lawyer tell you to expect, once you got the proceeding started?

Crystal: I could be sued for slander. Smythe could file a cross-complaint against me. He said I would really have to think about whether I was up to what I would have to go through. Basically, *I* would be on trial. It would be a grueling, painful experience.

Jim: I guess justice is a long way off.

Crystal: Justice is non-existent at this time.

Jim: There are a lot of people who cannot fathom it. Since I wrote my first book, which documents a lot about SRA, I have been interviewed on the radio by some well-meaning people who say, "We understand about multiple personality, but don't you think this satanic ritual abuse stuff must be fabricated or something? How can you even believe in it?"

So there I am live on the radio, and all I can say is that memory work sometimes brings up certain kinds of abuse, and sometimes brings up other kinds of abuse, but memory work is always the same. Whether it is abuse by a neighbor or a brother, whether it is seeing somebody being killed in front of you or feeling terror from a threatening family member, or whether it is a ritual, the process feels just the same. The first time you and I got into memory work, it didn't turn up SRA. It was wrenching. It was about Jerry Smythe . . .

Crystal: He was raping me in my own room, with my mother drunk in the next room.

Jim: And then a few months later, other memories started to come in, and it was SRA. They were both awful. They both seemed valid to me. Why should one be accepted and the other thrown out the window?

Crystal: I remember when the ritual abuse was going on. They always told me that "no one will ever believe you." And they were right. They knew. The things they did were so outlandish, they knew. People can't fathom it. They can't believe it. It is too much for the mind to even conceive. But it happens. There are kids living out there who are going through these things and having nightmares every night when they go to sleep.

Jim: Once that has happened, it cannot be changed. You can't ever erase it.

Crystal: No. It can't be taken away. I have the hope now that God can make my life different from now on. I didn't have that hope before, that I could ever live a happy life. God has given me people to love me, people I feel safe with. It took me a long time to get to that point, but still, it will never go away. You can't ever forget the pain, the horror of it all.

Jim: You had been in therapy with me for over a year before we even started the memory work. How long had you been depressed before that time?

Crystal: My whole life. I couldn't remember a time I was not depressed.

Jim: You became a Christian about ten years ago. After you met God, how did that change things?

Crystal: It didn't take away the depression. I just felt hopeful. I could feel Jesus' presence with me. It was somebody safe, and somebody who gave me the hope that things would be okay. But there were these parts in me that were locked away, that didn't have any hope, so the depression didn't go away until the memories were brought out, and God had a chance to put His hand on it. He restored life to those parts, and it's been integrating slowly, part by part.

The depression actually got worse when I started doing the memory work. It has been a long, hard process, but it does work. I used to wonder a lot, Does it ever end? It sure didn't feel like it. But it does, after the memories have received healing.

Jim: You know, you are one of the few people I know of who did memory work, and didn't drop out of therapy two or three times!

Crystal: It was my only hope. I had tried everything else to get healing to make my life right, and I really believe God brought me to a therapist who wanted Him to be a part of my therapy. It was my last hope of getting through it, of changing my life. So if I gave that up, it was like giving everything up completely.

Jim: That is sobering. You had come to the end of the rope and you had to hang on. When we first met, you were not on very good terms with your family.

Crystal: One thing in therapy was learning how to protect myself, and how to speak up. That was something I had never been allowed to do growing up. If I spoke up against Smythe, I would be beaten and raped. It was traumatizing. I would shake after standing up for myself.

I finally came to the point in my therapy, though, where I was able to say to my family, "Look, this is what happened. This is the truth." Everything finally made sense to them. Just being around this man, they knew he was awful, but they had no idea how bad. The truth came out, and it is like God used the truth to glue the pieces of my family back together. It even caused my family to take a look at their own lives again in the light of reality, and it helped them a lot.

Jim: Now that is kind of nice. Instead of talking about the bad apple effect—where the whole barrel is lost—you are talking about just the opposite. A little sugar in the water sweetens the whole pitcher.

Crystal: Now they love me and value me even more. They are protective of me in a good sort of way. That's nice. I feel fortunate in that way. I know people whose families never do believe them. Their families are still alienated.

Jim: What about friendships?

Crystal: There was a big change for me in friendships. Some people can grow with you and other people can't. It was such a hard process to go through that I couldn't fight any battles other than what I was fighting. Some friendships just dissipated on their own when there was any conflict.

Jim: What about friendships in church?

Crystal: The best thing you can do for people is not to preach at them, or tell them they need to *do* anything. They need God to touch them. Just love them and accept them where they're at. Care for them as you would for somebody who's been through a tragic accident. Instead of trying to exert your spirituality over them, just put your love under them. It's the most godly thing you can do. Just support them in their therapy and in their healing. Believe for them when they can't. Use your faith for them.

Jim: Did you ever come to the point where you were losing your faith?

Crystal: I think I lost faith a lot. I don't ever remember thinking, *I'm not going to love God any more,* but the reality of my life was that there had been no one to help me. These people could walk in and do whatever they wanted to do. My life was like living in a tomb. It was just death and horror. It's hard to relive that, to know that was reality, and then to have people around me acting like "Suzy Christian." I lost hope a lot, but somehow God kept me going. He is faithful even when we're faithless.

There were times when I really did think about dying; it seemed that was the only answer. Even though God did not want that, these circumstances were so extreme that it seemed the only way out for me. It makes me think about another thing that becomes an issue sometimes with church people—antidepressants, medication to help the survivor through the bad times. That was frowned upon—you were using a "crutch" instead of using God. I think that's the furthest thing from the truth. I think God wants us to have all the help we can get. If an antidepressant will help us not to kill ourselves, I don't think He is opposed to it at all. That was an immense help to me. It really has gotten me through.

I remember people referring to it in a bad way, saying, "When I'm depressed, I just praise God, and that's my antidepressant." Praising God is a good thing, and sometimes it can take depression away, but these people haven't experienced the level of pain that survivors have. Their wounds don't go as deep and they don't bleed as much. We do need help—and antidepressants do help us. We can praise God and receive the extra help we need from the medicine, too.

Jim: What would you say to people about suicide?

Crystal: Don't do it. Somehow, God can work a miracle, and though we can't erase the past, He does have in store for us a future that's worth living. So don't let that be taken away from yourself. You've already been robbed of so much—don't let them rip that off from you, too.

Jim: What does your future look like now?

Crystal: It looks pretty good. God has reshaped my life. He's given me people who care about me, and I care about them. He has restored my mind. Having my brain back is an amazing thing. It's wonderful not to have that feeling of being violated. To have possession of your mind, your heart and your soul is what you want. They are the most important gifts God gave to you. To be given those things back is wonderful.

There wasn't anything the cultists didn't take away. They violated everything; they laid hold of and destroyed. I'm still going through some painful memories, but I know that going through those memories just leads to more wholeness for me.

Jim: You and I have talked about this a hundred times. I am always looking for the least painful way for healing, but I just can't figure out ways to make it less painful for you. It seems to be pretty awful.

Crystal: It is awful, but there's no way to get around it. You can't get to the other side. You have to go through it. I believe God can shorten the time and have His hand on the process, but you still have to go through it.

I think a lot of denial is still going on. The problem is so big for laymen—and so complicated in some ways—that they try to find some answers for SRA. They want some easy steps, but they just don't know. It turns out being more denial and more minimization, and then revictimization. I think that you must not pretend you have been trained or know what you are doing, or you will do more damage to the person. The survivor is hanging on to a thread of grace as it is, having survived it in the first place. So don't make it harder for them. Don't claim to be a doctor when you're not.

Jim: It is really not a measure of God's grace, whether the everyday kinds of solutions work or not. God is still very full of grace, and He wants to heal, but He doesn't do it in the usual ways for this kind of serious pain. Crystal, is your experience of God qualitatively different while you are in the middle of the deepest pain?

Crystal: I've seen God in such amazing ways through this process, in the way He comes to me in healing, and in the way He shows His compassion. I feel closer to Him. I feel like I understand more about His love for me, and for other people.

Jim: I wonder, if you hadn't gotten into the middle of these memories, if your walk with God would be as close as it is.

Crystal: Parts of me were locked away, and they had been told that God hated me. I could keep that closet door shut for my whole life, but what's in that closet will always be there. I had to open it. It feels much more now like a relationship with Him, and when I look at other people, I can see them more in the way He does.

Jim: What do you mean?

Crystal: I guess it's my heart—like God stepped into it, and it grew. When you've known the kind of pain and suffering I have known, you have a love for other people, a compassion for them, more understanding for them for whatever kind of suffering, whether physical or emotional. You just know what pain is, and you look at people more mercifully. What God cares about most is that we receive His life and His healing.

And it's okay for us to be angry. Being angry through this process is part of the healing. God is just as angry that it happened, and it's the right kind of anger because it was a very wrong thing that happened.

We don't need to tell people how to feel, what to feel, or when to feel it. That is not your job as a pastor or friend or someone being in church ministry. Feelings need to come up— the anger, the pain—they need to come to the surface so they can be dealt with. Being told that this feeling or that feeling is wrong, or that it is sin, only causes more damage. It reverses the healing process.

Jim: If you had been in a church where the people had not let you feel, or tried to make you stop your feelings, you would have gotten more and more depressed and less able to walk with God, and less able to appreciate people. None of those good things would have happened if you hadn't allowed yourself to have your feelings.

Crystal: It's really important in those circumstances, because the feelings often come before the memories. A lot of times these feelings would come, and then the memories would follow. If I have to stuff away my feelings, I'm never going to put them together with the memories, and the truth isn't going to come, and the healing won't happen.

Jim: Well, I am for healing! It's a great joy for me to see that God has done good things for you, and you're moving on.

Crystal: It makes me want to turn around, look behind me, and put out my hand to the one who is coming through next.

Jim: There is no shortage of people who are suffering. I believe your story will encourage other people to get into the position where they can turn around, and put out their hand to still others who have gone through serious suffering.

8

CHRISTINA: SRA Uncovered*

AT THE END of a conference on MPD last fall, Christina was the last person to come by to talk with me. She was gentle and soft-spoken when she introduced herself. "I am a nurse, and I wanted to hear what you had to say this weekend. I am one of the people you have been speaking about."

We spent a few minutes talking, and she encouraged me by saying that her experience was totally consistent with the approach I advocated. She had not read anything I wrote, so her treatment experience was not influenced by my material. I knew then that she could provide some important information I had been looking for—psychological and spiritual involvement in MPD therapy, with "complete, stable integration." As we talked, I soon realized her story had been kept secret too long. Her quiet determination to become healthy and her abundant love for others assured me she is a person others can look up to as a role model, a person of compassion.

Christina: I originally got into therapy because of nightmares. I was a Christian at the time, in my mid-20s, and I was having some pretty bad nightmares that would not go away. I had prayed; I had read my Bible; I had done many things to try to get rid of them. I couldn't work because I was losing so much

---

* A more thorough discussion about satanic ritual abuse appears in *Uncovering the Mystery of MPD* by James G. Friesen, Ph.D. See "Suggested Reading List" on page 224 of this book.

sleep, so I called up a psychotherapist here in my city. He was teaching a seminary class on biblical counseling, and that's how I knew him. I asked him if he ever saw students from seminary, and he said he did.

Jim: You were a student in seminary at the time?

Christina: Yes.

Jim: You are a nurse now. Why did you go to seminary?

Christina: When I entered seminary, I originally wanted to help people work through emotional pain, but I was very unaware of what was going on inside of me. Looking back on it now, I was really trying to resolve some of my own pain, most of it unconscious, I think.

Jim: People in that position would get into some kind of a program designed specifically toward healing. Is that the kind of program you gravitated toward at seminary?

Christina: Yes, biblical counseling. I really wanted to help other people, and I found myself always sensing other people's pain very easily. I would feel it very clearly. Later I discovered that other people's pain was really touching my own. Anyway, during the time I was taking the very first class in that curriculum, I made the counseling appointment. He asked me some questions, and I discovered in the first session that I was petrified, and I didn't understand why I was so frightened. I went in and started describing some of the dreams. We began to build trust with one another during those early sessions. In a session early in therapy, I looked down at my watch and noticed the session was over, and he asked me if I remembered doing this or saying that. I didn't know what he was talking about. I had "lost some time."

Jim: Was losing time a regular occurrence for you, or was this a brand new thing?

Christina: It was a regular occurrence, but I would chalk it up to bad memory. I would think, *I'm just not with it today. I can't remember anything.* Sometimes I was afraid something was really wrong with me, and I thought that if I just ignored it, it might go away. In the first session, the counselor asked some interesting questions. For example: Did I have clothing in any closets that I didn't remember buying? Frankly, I lied to him at the time. I knew it was true, but I had not figured it out yet. I thought, *Well, if I figure out some day why I have clothes in my closets that I don't remember buying, then I can talk about it.* But I was afraid to tell anybody. I was just afraid I would be marked as crazy or something, so I didn't tell him then. I only got into therapy because of the nightmares, and I thought, *Okay, it will be a few sessions. We will find out why I am having them. We will deal with the problem and I will be fine.* I had no idea it would turn into five years, but I'm glad it did. I began to uncover different events, different experiences. Alters ranging from age 4 all the way to age 23 began to come out.

I'm trying to think of what it was like while I was in therapy. I experienced both good feelings and hell at the same time. Many times I literally thought I was going to die in the session. The feelings were so intense as I went back into the experience. The alters would come out, and we would agree to look at what happened, and then the actual feelings of the experience would become very much alive. Not only would I feel the emotional pain, but I also would feel some of the physical sensations—and they made me very frightened of going any further in therapy.

Jim: Christina, I was just wondering, did he label that experience for you? Did he say that's an abreaction or that's a flashback or anything like that?

Christina: No. The first couple of months in therapy he didn't introduce any of the phrases that you and I are familiar with now.

Jim: No explanations?

Christina: Not initially. He didn't plant ideas in me. The more we talked, the more I felt safe to talk about some things that I consciously had always remembered. It was in talking about some of those conscious things that some of the unconscious began coming out. It was after some undeniable evidence of MPD began "leaking out" in the sessions, that we talked about the possibility of MPD.

Jim: But had you ever had that kind of a reliving experience before therapy?

Christina: No.

Jim: So it only started when you were in therapy?

Christina: Exactly.

Jim: Did that make you wonder about therapy? That maybe there was something weird going on? Or maybe he was doing crazy things to you, or introducing ideas into your head?

Christina: No, he didn't introduce any ideas, but I was frightened at first because things I had been able to control previously began "coming out of me." Even so, there were parts of me that wanted to stay. The crazy thing is, I thought most people had voices in their heads like that. I thought it was normal, that everybody had these little parts of themselves. I just accepted that. *You mean everybody is not like this? Other people don't lose time? Don't they all have voices in their heads?* I thought I was crazy. But he was very good at laying a foundation of trust, and that created an environment of safety. That safety helped me begin to talk more, and the alters began to feel safe, and they began to come out more.

Jim: Okay. So, in therapy, it was both hell and wonderful?

Christina: It was wonderful in the sense that I felt I was finally with someone I could trust, someone who understood what was happening and did not reject me and did not label me as dirty, or as a horrible person who simply was no good.

I have to say that we spent a lot of time laying that foundation of trust. In looking back on it, I realize it was a critical part of therapy. That foundation enabled me to let go of a lot of things, and to talk about my fear of being abandoned or betrayed or abused. Frankly, I was a frightened little girl!

I look back, and I think to myself, *I should have died,* and then I ask God, "Why *didn't* I die? Why *did* I survive? Why did I live when others died? Why were others sacrificed and I wasn't?" Initially, I would have some feelings of guilt, thinking *Well, I would have died if I hadn't agreed to do some things.* Then I have to do some healthy self-talk, and remind myself that I was only 5, and when they said they would cut my heart out, I believed them. It all makes sense now.

Fear and confusion were two emotions that dominated my life. They were like old friends that I carried into therapy, and it took a lot of work to stop connecting those feelings to the therapy.

Jim: As a youngster, around 5, you went through some experiences of satanic ritual abuse?

Christina: Yes.

Jim: And you had no idea about it when you got into therapy, but then it started to emerge?

Christina: The only thing I remembered was an incident when I was 14, with one of my mother's boyfriends. He had attempted to molest me. I told my mother about it, and she believed *him,* so nothing was ever done about it. That's the only bad thing I could remember from my childhood. But I began doing things in therapy and feeling emotions that I couldn't connect to an experience. All the emotion was there, but the experience was missing.

Jim: You mean the fear and confusion were around you?

Christina: Yes.

Jim: But you had no idea where they had come from?

Christina: Right.

Jim: And you found they had come from the early experiences of the ritual abuse?

Christina: Yes.

Jim: How did you finally make the connection between the emotions and the original SRA events?

Christina: My nightmares consisted mainly of black robes, fire, blood and screams. I would wake up trembling in a cold sweat. Also, the alters began coming out in therapy, and I became conscious of them. The feelings and the experiences came together when I would talk to the alter and tell her that it was safe to talk—she was holding the experience from me. It had been her job, but I convinced her it was safe to tell me now. When she began to tell me, I began not only to see the experience, but also to feel some of the physical sensations of it. That's when the connection would occur between the experience and the feeling. I would begin feeling those things, and literally owning them.

That's when the alter would become integrated. I don't believe this could have happened without knowing that it was "safe" in the room, and a "safe" person was reminding me, "You are not there any more. It is not happening to you again. That is in the past."

Jim: You know, fear and confusion sometimes have their spiritual components. Was there a sense of spiritual warfare or spiritual healing that went on for you during your therapy time?

Christina: Yes, absolutely! Many times I would feel extremely cold—the room became extremely cold. I would tell my therapist what was happening, and that I felt there were demons in the room. My therapist is a Christian who understands spiritual warfare, and together we would begin rebuking the demons that were in the room. Then I would feel the coldness leave.

I remember distinctly trying to get in touch with a particular experience that we knew an alter held. We knew a little about the experience, but she had not revealed it all to me. I felt a strong sense of warfare in the room. Particularly—I know this sounds strange—I distinctly remember the smell of sulfur. When I was in college, I was good in chemistry and I remember doing experiments that involved ammonia and sulfur. I remembered that smell from college, and I thought, *well, this must be a memory from college days.* Now I know it wasn't. It was further back than that: It was from the rituals.

I remember smelling sulfur; I remember the burning. I remember the colors of blue and green and yellow, and I remember the altars. I remember them being very cold. Oftentimes the rituals violated things that I now consider very special and sacred. For example, the phrase, "In the name of the Father, Son and Holy Spirit," was violated. In one particular ritual where I was on the altar at 6 years old, I was raped—I don't know how to say this except exactly as it is—with each penetration, the satanist would say, "In the name of the Father, the Son and the Holy Spirit." They would inflict the pain and the abuse, and connect it deliberately to sacred things. That is why, as therapy progressed, it became very difficult to pray in church. It became very difficult to hear those words, as this particular experience was being approached in therapy.

Jim: That makes sense.

Christina: It made a lot of sense. It was very painful and very hard, and many times in therapy I would beg God to please take me home because I feared I would get through this process and end up hating Him, not loving Him. But I wanted to keep clinging to Him. I felt like no matter what happened, He was the only one I could totally trust and the only one who had the answers. He was the only one who knew my deepest needs, and I knew He could meet them.

Jim: So did you find that God was a help to you during therapy, or was He sort of uninvolved?

Christina: He was at the core of it. Many a night I would cry out to Him, "Why did You allow this to happen if You claim to be God? You had the power not to allow it to happen."

He would answer, "Can I trust you with this experience even if you never know why?"

I couldn't help but fall at His feet in prayer, because something deep down inside me knew He held the answer; He was right. If I let go of Him, I would let go of me, and I would let go of any true help. Many nights Satan would try to convince me I belonged to him; there was no hope for me; I was dedicated to him. He would whisper to me that I was damaged goods; no one would want me in marriage; no one would understand; no one would believe me. The fear that no one would believe me was very strong. I felt I would be hanging myself if I talked.

But God was at the core of therapy, not only being the one I could safely rant and rave to, but also the one who stayed there and comforted me in the darkness. The Holy Spirit would come to me in the night and would draw me "out of deep water." Verse 16 in Psalm 18 says that "He sent from on high, He took me; He drew me out of many waters." I would hold on to that verse, because I believed He was doing that for me. I didn't think I could trust anybody completely except Him. So I held on to Him even when I thought, *Why did You let it happen? You claim You love me. Why did You let it happen?* Sometimes I would feel a strange sense of awe that this almighty God created me, but at the same time

I'd wonder, *What's going on in His mind? He says He loves me and yet He allowed these things to happen. What is He doing with my life?*

Still, I felt a sense of security in that I have a mighty God who is intimately involved in my life. That sounds strange I know, but that's literally how it was. There were times I felt very close to Him, in spite of what I was going through, but there were also times I felt far away from Him.

Jim: Did you ever come up with a resolution of that conflict, of that tension about how a wonderful God could let these awful things happen to you?

Christina: I discovered through these experiences that this mighty God was *not* standing in the corner with His hands tied behind His back, watching them do this to me. Rather, He was on the altar, also—He was on the cross, also. He was beaten and bloodied, and horribly abused on the cross, and He knew each pain and each feeling. I look at what I went through and see myself as one who has an opportunity to identify just a little bit more with what Christ went through, and therefore I have come closer to Him.

I know a God who is well acquainted with grief—the man of sorrows that the Scriptures talk about. I know a God now who is able to comfort in a way I have never known before. His comfort is real, and it reaches to the core of me. It's not superficial. It's not just a bunch of words that people are supposed to say when they are hurting. He really is there. He really is real, and He is able to heal. He is able to comfort. He was able to clean up all the blood. He was able to close all my wounds that were oozing, the wounds that were still bleeding. Now I have just scars on my body and I have memories, but they are scars that represent a testimony of the saving power of God. I don't know how else to say it, except that healing is possible. Healing is real, and everything Satan meant for evil, God can turn around for good.

I see Him now as my Creator who painfully allowed the abuse to occur, because He could see what lay ahead for me. I don't believe I could have known the depths of His love if the suffering had not happened. I chose to hold on to Him because I knew no one else could fill the vacuum in my life. So I held on, and I cried, and I saw a living God touch me in a way I will never forget.

I used to think that I would always have a broken mind, a broken body and a broken spirit. God has mended each of those. The "mending" came with seeing Him "torn"—I identified with His suffering. I'm learning a lot about life now. I feel about ten years behind emotionally, because I'm experiencing things I never had an opportunity to experience before. For example, I'm in my 30s, but to interact with men in a way that's not frightening is very new to me. I am learning things about relationships that most 18-year-olds already know. I am just now getting around to understanding dating and how to relate socially and not be petrified of the opposite sex.

Jim: A few minutes ago you said that God has been able to turn those things that were so horrifying and awful into good. Just what is your post therapy life like these days? How is that good showing up in your life?

Christina: Well, now I'm a registered nurse at a hospital. I work with cancer patients. This is my third degree. I originally studied geology because I love the sciences. My college years were kind of crazy, where I would do very well in chemistry one quarter, and then do very bad the next quarter, and as I understood later on, I had different alters during different quarters. Some were smart in chemistry and some weren't. That was kind of humorous to me, looking back on it.

Jim: What about biblical counseling?

Christina: That was next. I finished the seminary degree a few years ago. Then I got into nursing because it combined my love for the sciences with my need for involvement with people, and so I work with patients on a cancer floor. In working with these patients I have a lot of opportunity to intervene, not only with the patients but also with their families, in the grief process. There is a lot of grief. There is a lot of pain. There is a lot of not only emotional pain, but also physical pain.

I remember one patient the night he was dying, and this man was a Christian. I went to his bedside before our shift was over. I knew he would not last through the night, and I remember leaning over him and looking into his eyes because he was unable to speak by this time. But he was still conscious and he could look at me.

I looked into his eyes, and inside of me I asked God, "What can I do for this man?" There was nothing I could do by way of treatment, nothing medically I could do any more for him. All I could see in his eyes was a lot of fear, and I thought to myself, *That's so familiar*—the terror I saw in his eyes. He knew he was dying, and I remembered the terror I felt when I was being abused and I would pray to God, "Let me die." I asked, "What can I say to him, God?"

And God told me to tell him, "Don't be afraid. God's arms are safe."

And then I realized that those were living words for *me*. I had discovered that God's arms were safe. Because His arms were safe for me, I could offer this man the same hope. He died later that night, leaving cancer behind. Looking back on that experience I thought, *That's something Satan can't touch. It's something he cannot abuse. It's something he cannot distort. It's something he cannot take away from me—the safe arms of God*. The way the Holy Spirit ministered to the patient that night was something Satan cannot touch. That same kind of ministry to me by the Holy Spirit while I was in therapy made all the difference in the world. God would minister to me in ways that Satan could not touch.

Jim: You know, it amazes me that after all you have been through, you can be right in the middle of the same kind of experience, without losing it!

Christina: That *is* amazing! In nursing school, I lost it a little bit. I would have a lot of flashbacks, especially when I went through pediatrics, where I would be taking care of babies in the nursery. A baby was killed in one of the rituals that I was in, where the knife was in my hand, and the adult behind me had his arms around me with his hands over my hands on the knife, and . . .

Jim: Believe me, I have heard that scene described by so many people. It's very real.

Christina: I am wondering if they were also drugged. I know I was drugged—given shots in my leg, and then taken away. I felt like I was in a dream. I would feel very weak and unable to fight.

Jim: That's also familiar. There's no resistance when you are drugged like that. There is no fighting. You just survive.

Christina: Anyway, it is amazing to me that I'm able to do what I do now, because I'm in coding situations.

Jim: "Code blue"—a critical life-and-death situation.

Christina: Yes. Of course, they call it different things in different hospitals.

Jim: My wife works in a hospital, and is called into coding situations.

Christina: I did have one flashback with one lady that we coded, where we had to put electrode pads on her chest to get a rhythm. She had a beautiful blue nightgown on and the night-gown was designed in such a way that we could not pull it up or down, and I literally had to take my hands and rip it down the middle. And I had a flashback of my own clothing being torn in a particular experience, and what was amazing to me is that I didn't lose it during the code—I continued doing what had to be done in order to work with her.

It wasn't until after it was all over that I noticed I was trembling—and I was remembering that experience. And once again, God came to me at the time of my need. He said, "You are not there anymore. They ripped your clothes and they hurt you, but it's okay, because I'm the Great Physician, and I'm healing you. And they can't touch who you are. They did a lot to your body, but they can't touch who you are. You belong to me."

I had an alter named Carolyn. She had memorized lots of Scripture, which is how I think God was in the core of so much of this. This alter knew all these Scriptures, and I don't remember memorizing any of them, but she would quote one of my favorite passages in John 10: "I give them eternal life, and they shall never perish; no one can snatch them out of my hand. My Father, who has given them to me, is greater than all; no one can snatch them out of my Father's hand" [verses 28,29]. I would remember that verse. Carolyn would bring it to mind. Now that she is integrated, I remember them all—in my own consciousness—all the verses she memorized. And God reminded me of that verse, after that code, that no one is able to snatch me up.

Sometimes I wonder, *Is there ever going to be a time when it doesn't hurt anymore? When the flashbacks don't occur anymore?* Yes. There will be. Some experiences I had are pure memory now. They don't have the physical or emotional sensations connected with them.

There are other memories I still sometimes have flashbacks to, but the effect of the flashback becomes less and less each time it happens. And that's because I apply truth to it. I remind myself what the truth is, and the memory loses its power. I try to tell myself that when old coping mechanisms want to kick in, especially suicidal feelings. The suicidal ideation was like an old familiar friend. I had been trained to think of suicide whenever I thought of the experiences, considered them, wanted to talk about them, or wanted to feel them. So the old suicidal feelings would come and it was literally like an old friend. And so, when I would have flashbacks . . .

Jim: Just a second. You mean satanists *programmed* you to become suicidal if you would even *think* of telling anybody about the rituals?

Christina: Oh, yes! I haven't talked to them since I was a child. I haven't confronted my abusers, except one. So I haven't been able to ask them anything. I doubt they would tell me anyway. I think they were hoping I would just kill myself and that would protect the secret, but God had other plans. I very happily tell the secret now. Unfortunately, there are many who don't want to believe people can do those things.

Jim: Have you been fairly open in talking about your experiences?

Christina: With certain people. I have brothers and sisters who have not gotten in touch with things yet. Some are living very dysfunctional lives because they are still guarding secrets.

Jim: You think they all went through the same things that you did?

Christina: Not all of them. My younger brother did. Most of my older siblings have not given me any indication that they went through anything like this. My oldest sister has given some information about her own abusive experience, but she has not revealed any SRA. My younger brother and I have talked, and he has told me about some things, but he gets very anxious if we talk too much. Things just kick in with him, so I have to walk carefully with him.

Jim: But when you talk about it to others, they have a hard time believing it?

Christina: Yes. They have a hard time believing it because they look at me, and they think, *But you are still here. You are alive. If all this really happened, why are you still alive?* They don't say that, but I can see the puzzlement on their face. I have been very careful about who I share it with. There are members of my family who were involved in satanic abuse, but I do not live near them anymore. They are still alive, and they might still be active, so I have to be careful about *whom* I tell, just out of consideration for my brothers and sisters.

Jim: That makes good sense to me.

Christina: But regarding others I have told, I have gotten mixed reactions. Most of them have been good. Most of them have been very supportive and very believing. Some have said they believe me, but they have been kind of aloof to me, not talking to me as they used to; I think out of fear of what more they might hear. And I think it is just their own fear. They can't handle something like that. They can't come to grips with the fact that human beings can do those kinds of things.

Jim: You know, from the times I have talked with you, I'm stunned that you can go through that kind of a life, and want to get back into it just to help people as a cancer nurse. I think if I had gone through that kind of thing, I might want to be a barkeeper on the Love Boat. That's what I'd be! I'd never want to think about it again, and maybe I'd drown my sorrows every chance I got! But what's amazing to me is that you jumped right back into it to help people. That takes not only courage, but also more stamina and will power than I can imagine.

Christina: That is because of what God did for me in the process. That's why I said God was in the core of therapy. If I had not allowed Him to be in the core of the therapy, none of this could have happened. He made me stronger. Not only was He healing me, but He also was making me into a warrior instead of a victim. That's why I prefer not to use the word *victim* anymore. It gives ground to Satan. I'm not a victim now.

Jim: It seems to me that your position as a nurse not only combines science and counseling, as you were suggesting from your university background, but it also gives you a "hands on" opportunity to know people in more than just an emergency situation—at times of life and death and grief and struggling. Your power has been magnified a hundred times greater than what has been inflicted on you, as far as I can tell.

Christina: Satan's purpose in all of the abuse was to kill, steal and destroy. I think it is a horror to Satan to see me stronger and closer to God as a result of the pain, rather than his intended purpose of destruction.

One of the things I notice experiencing on the nursing floor is a freedom to, in a sense, walk back into the darkness. But I'm walking back into the darkness as an adult, as a woman, empowered by the Holy Spirit, and as a woman who has healing. Not as a woman with something in her hands to hurt, nor as a woman fearfully walking into the darkness expecting to be hurt. I'm walking in to relieve some hurt. That's fulfilling for me, and it's encouraging. One of the things I remember which helped me "get into life and live," and not let the past imprison me, was remembering that it's the *life* and not the pain of abuse that's going to go on. If, in therapy, I started thinking, *This pain will never end,* that's when I would get suicidal, and that's when I would think I can't go on. But when I started remembering that it was life that was going to go on—not the pain—*that* helped me. And I remember I'm in present-day post therapy; I'm living life, because life is what's going on. Not the pain. Satan would like me to think the pain will never end, but he is good at lying.

Jim: Now I need to ask you a couple of "mandatory" questions. Little tiny ones. Okay? For example, how long were you in therapy? Four years of treatment?

Christina: No. Five years.

Jim: How long since you have been out?

Christina: About a year.

Jim: Any evidence of falling apart since then, or did the personalities stick?

Christina: Certain anniversaries during the year are hard, because those were times when some of the most violent things happened. But each passing anniversary has less and less effect on me, and I get stronger and stronger. As far as, did it stick? Yes. It sticks. It sticks with the glue of the Holy Spirit. It sticks very well. I talk to my therapist occasionally on the phone, about how things are going. I've gone back to see him occasionally to talk about some things that are new to me—just a lot of "how to" stuff. Sometimes we talk about struggles that come with living a "new life," things I never experienced or understood, and I need a little help with.

Jim: Was there any evidence of demons delivered from you during treatment?

Christina: Yes. Yes, there were. I experienced demonic oppression during some sessions.

Jim: Do you have a sense of how many, or does that even cross your mind?

Christina: No, it doesn't. I didn't count. There were sessions where I felt like I was choking, sessions where I felt like I was being held down, literally, by something I couldn't see, and then I would be freed from them. They didn't come back, because we were careful to pray, and not leave "the house vacant" for the demons to come back and oppress me by way of that memory as an "open door" to them.

Jim: Did you ever have any trouble figuring out the difference between alters and demons?

Christina: Initially I did. This is where God comes in—I began to ask Him to teach me what the difference is. Also my therapist and I talked about the differences and similarities between alters and demons, and how to recognize them.

Jim: And did any of the demons ever come back because they were alters in the first place?

Christina: No.

Jim: It's been a year—and no evidence of that?

Christina: No. No, because I belong to Christ. I don't mean to sound flippant. That's not how I meant it.

Jim: It's a fact. That's the way I look at it.

Christina: Sometimes I'm not on my guard and I allow demonic oppression to get the best of me. But when I rebuke the demons in the name of Christ, they leave. And frankly, I don't think they can stand being around me much anymore. I really believe the only power that Satan has is going to be through my belief in his lies. And when that's eradicated, then he is so powerless it's pitiful. I take him seriously as being the spiritual being of darkness, and I take his power seriously, but I take even more seriously God's power, and I exercise that. That defeats the power of Satan.

If I had to say anything at the end of this conversation, it would be to those who are still in therapy, to just stand on the truth and don't let the experience or the battle remove you from it, because it works. The fierceness of the battle is not evidence of defeat. Always remember that. There's a mighty God there who is in control of it all. The suffering doesn't mean that God has stopped loving us. A powerful healing can come out of our woundedness if we will allow it. Hold on to the One who will never abandon you.

9

PAULA:
Intensive
Therapy

Jim: Your psychologist and I were on the phone, and he told me about how you had compressed a lot of therapy into a few months, with, what seems to me, very favorable results. You went through treatment pretty quickly at his hospital. I don't work in a hospital setting, so your experience was probably a little different from what I usually see. How many times have you been hospitalized altogether?

Paula: I would have to guess—16 to 18 times is about right, but only the last two helped with the MPD at all. I got the correct diagnosis four years ago, but no one would work with that diagnosis here. I live in a small town, and the MPD just scared the therapists around here. I eventually went to a Christian psychiatric hospital for MPD last summer, but that was in another state.

Jim: What happened in the other hospitals?

Paula: Basically, all they did was medicate me until I was a zombie, or put me in a padded room. One time in a hospital they put me in leather restraints for three and a half days straight.

Jim: What happened during that time—did you just stay in a child personality in the restraints?

Paula: I think it was one of the older personalities, who was very angry.

Jim: So you were furious for three days straight? That does not sound exactly therapeutic!

Paula: And they put me on a lot of Thorazine in that particular hospital. [Thorazine is an anti-psychotic medication, used for schizophrenia.]

Jim: What were they hospitalizing you for?

Paula: Depression, suicidal tendencies, manic depressive, schizoid personality, paranoid schizophrenia. Every label we could think of I've had put on me, so I don't know the exact label they had then.

Jim: Were the hospitals checking on the previous diagnoses to be sure they were working on the right thing, or were they thinking the other hospitals just had the wrong diagnosis?

Paula: They went from scratch each time. No one ever checked back with the other hospitals. Maybe it was because one was in England and the others were in five different states here in the U.S., but each time the doctors decided they would do their own evaluation.

Jim: And they came up with different diagnoses each time! So after that many bad experiences in hospitals, you must have been pretty burned out on them.

Paula: I felt hopeless. I was sure they didn't know what they were talking about and they thought I was basically crazy.

Jim: What were you in the hospital for the first time?

Paula: They said it was post-partum depression, after my first child was born. They gave me Thorazine. There were all men in that hospital, except one other girl. At one point I was medicated so deeply, they had to have someone in my room 24 hours a day, and they fed me with an I.V. for a whole week. Sometimes I went through shock treatments.

About eighteen months after I had been put in the leather restraints, I was pregnant with my second child, and my husband and the doctor decided I was not capable of carrying that child so they did an abortion. It was old enough to know that it would have been a little girl. Then I got really depressed, and they gave me shock treatments again.

Jim: With all that in your background, it must have been hard to consider going back into any hospital.

Paula: When they suggested this Christian setting, it was kind of humorous. I went to every person who had given me any kind of support, and told them this new doctor is wrong, and I'm not going there. I begged them all, and told them that I didn't need to go. I rode my bike about ten miles to see one person, and told him, "Please tell them I don't need to go!" But they all knew I needed something, so they said to go.

After I walked into the locked unit there and while I was waiting for them to begin, tears started rolling down my face because I was so afraid. I didn't believe they would do anything different. My thinking was, *I wonder what new kind of torture they have invented since the last time I was hospitalized!* Then two therapists came in to greet me, one male and one female. I panicked. It was like I was waiting to be punished. When they walked in the door, I was afraid it was a set-up!

Jim: What kind of a set-up?

Paula: I don't know! [Laughs] It was because of past experiences. But these people were so kind! I couldn't believe that the nurses would even pray with me. After a day or so, it changed my mind completely about how a hospital should be. Then we started into intensive therapy.

Jim: So what did you have to do to find the right doctor?

Paula: I started in therapy with a pastor in this town, who had worked with people regarding demon possession. He was studying ritual abuse and MPD, and he started working with me. He got to a point where he said, "It's getting dangerous for me to keep on working with you," because he had no hospital privileges or anything. He found a hospital where they could work with MPD from a Christian perspective. I was on disability and qualified for hospitalization there, and that's where my psychologist started working with me.

Jim: Did they already have the diagnosis at that time?

Paula: Of course. But they ran all the psychological tests and everything again. They knew when I went there that MPD was the diagnosis. So they verified it, and then they started working on it.

Jim: So did you have to move to the new state?

Paula: I went there only for the hospitalization. I have been hospitalized two separate times there, once for twenty-eight days and once for thirty-eight days. We did therapy six or eight hours a day, and sometimes even longer, because we knew it would be difficult any other way, unless I would move down there.

Jim: In the new city, did you have to develop another set of friends and another support network?

Paula: Just the nurses and the psychiatric technicians, who were tremendously supportive. I was in the hospital the whole time I was there. I didn't spend any time out. I came home in between the two stays. The psychologist has been consulting with my therapist here in between times. They have been working together.

Jim: And during your in-patient work, there were more than eighty personalities integrated, and more than 200 evil spirits were expelled?

Paula: Right. The psychologist says the reason we were able to progress so fast was that I had a personal relationship with Christ, a good biblical background, and that I was very intelligent. I don't know if that really had anything to do with the progress, but that's what he said.

Jim: I think people who can use this defense, dissociation, have to be intelligent, or they can't even use it in the first place.

Paula: That's true. I would agree with you 100 percent, but I have never met anyone else with MPD, or sat down and talked with them.

Jim: You are a loner in that respect?

Paula: I think that part of it is difficult. That's why I think it's exciting that you are writing a book. There have to be other people who are in the same situation, who are petrified and don't know where to turn.

Jim: That is very true, and many of them are looking for treatment that will start from both the spiritual and the psychological frameworks. I know that was true in your case, when you finally got to the intensive MPD work. One thing I want to do here is to see how MPD therapy works in other settings, so I would like to compare notes, okay? What would you tell your friends, or what would you want your friends to know, if you would be starting all over again? How could they help you?

Paula: I guess the biggest thing would be to not tell me I was lying all the time. You know, friends would say stuff that I hadn't said, as far as I was concerned. I didn't know I had said it. One of the alters had said it, and my friends would become angry, and then they wouldn't be my friends anymore. People need to be more understanding, and accept the fact that when a person has MPD he doesn't know what the other alters are saying any of the time. I did not know what any of the alters had said, until after the fact when somebody would tell me. People would quit being my friends real fast. That hurt more than anything.

Jim: That had been happening to you for quite a while?

Paula: Yes.

Jim: So as far as you were concerned, you couldn't figure out why people were always accusing you of lying?

Paula: Right. Even back in high school. After I went through the integration sessions, I finally made sense of what went on in high school. I had a close-knit group of friends, and one day they came up to me and said they were not ever going to speak to me again. I said, "Why? What have I done?"

They said, "You know what you have done, and you are no longer our friend." So for the rest of the junior and senior years of high school they were not my friends. I was alone. And to this day I don't know what I did, exactly, that upset them. At least I finally understand why they rejected me.

Jim: That must have been staggering, coming out of the blue like that. You had no idea what they were talking about. How shattering! And you suffered from that all the rest of the way through high school.

Paula: So that's what I would tell a person who knows someone who has MPD—believe her (or him) when she says she doesn't know what she did. Or if she doesn't show up on time, don't throw big fits.

Jim: Certain personalities might not want to be there, so you end up being late?

Paula: Right. Another thing: People would come by my house and ask, "Why did you move your furniture again?" I would get so frustrated because these people had known the diagnosis. I'd say, "Well, you know how it is. People just have to clean!" Or I would make something up. Or I would make a joke about it. I think I got hurt after a while, and maybe angry or afraid to let anybody know what was going on.

Jim: Evidently. When you got into treatment, did you have at least one or two people you learned to depend on, or who got interested and gave you the kind of consideration you needed?

Paula: Not in my family. There was my former therapist and his wife, a fireman and his family, and another couple in the church—those were the three couples. They stuck with it. They read some things about MPD, and they all tried to understand and help. They listened to my psychologist. They tried their best to support what was going on, and to understand and encourage, and that helped a lot. I didn't feel quite so alone. But mainly that was only after I had been hospitalized for MPD.

Jim: So help has come only within the last few months?

Paula: Yes.

Jim: What kind of things did these people do for you that helped most?

Paula: Out of all the things they helped with, I think the telephone calls were the most helpful. They let me call any time. I would get confused, because all of a sudden I was here, or I was some place else, and I would call them and they would bring me home.

Jim: So you had their phone numbers with you?

Paula: Yes. Usually I carried stuff in my pockets, or I had the numbers in my head. This is not that big a town. I think the telephone was the most important thing they helped with.

Jim: I wonder if there was a sense that God had prepared them, or somehow directed them to you?

Paula: Most of them said something had happened in their lives already, or they would never have understood. One couple said specifically that they didn't understand at all, but they felt God had made me a blessing to them so that they could help me. Does that make sense?

Jim: Oh, yes.

Paula: The other couple said the same thing. They said, "You don't realize how much it blesses us to help you, even though we don't fully understand. God has brought us to this position so we can be a benefit to you."

Jim: That's terrific.

Paula: And my pastor said he had learned so much working with me that it's going to give him the ability to work with others.

Jim: It's so reassuring to hear from you that you see God's hand in a lot of different ways—not only in preparing the people to help you, but in teaching your therapist things that will help others, and in bringing you all of these people who were absolutely crucial for your recovery.

Paula: And it seemed like every one of them came into focus at exactly the right time. You know, God's timing is exact—every one of them has come into my life at the crucial moment that they could help—even my psychologist. I could have had a lot of different therapists, but he happened to be the one who was more involved in MPD. And he said it had increased his faith as he saw how much healing happened through God.

Jim: You said that God, or that your knowledge of the Bible, or spiritual things had prepared you for this?

Paula: I was raised in church, and I married a man in the Navy who became a minister. I was a minister's wife for more than fifteen years, so I did a lot of teaching. I even had taught in a Christian women's organization. I have done a lot of Bible studies, and so I know a lot about the Bible. But I always felt that it didn't apply to what was wrong with me. I couldn't understand what was wrong with me, but I still believed God was there, and that He answered prayer. I just didn't know what to do for myself.

Jim: So all those years of Bible study . . .

Paula: They gave me the knowledge.

Jim: Gave you knowledge that would be needed later, but didn't pinpoint exactly what was wrong?

Paula: Right. You know, I didn't find the answer to what was wrong, and I didn't find the answer to how to fix it until God used other people to show me, and *then* He used the knowledge He had already given me.

Jim: But it took a while?

Paula: Oh, yes. It took a long while.

Jim: And were you still married to the preacher when you found out about the MPD?

Paula: Yes, I was, but for only a few months, and then I divorced him. That was four years ago. I divorced him because he was abusive. He was a different man when the door closed.

Jim: Too bad. That was a trap—you were living with terror, and nobody would believe their pastor was abusive, so there was practically nothing you could do.

Paula: It was abusive enough that it created some of the alters! I had an automobile accident and was raped by one of the medics, and my husband was abusive during my recovery. I decided I didn't want to go through that anymore, so I divorced him. He remarried shortly thereafter. But the diagnosis was four years ago, the accident was a couple of months after the diagnosis, and a couple of months after that I divorced him. After that I went into a different religion for a couple of years.

Jim: What was that like?

Paula: It was very difficult. I went as far as a single woman can in that religion, because I thought maybe there were answers there. When you first go into that religion they only teach you a few things. Well, I learned more than even the local leader knew, and I found the fallacy of it. It took quite a bit to get out of that religion, once I had gone that far.

Jim: What did you see to be the fallacy?

Paula: One fallacy is that they don't think you can have real true salvation. There's no peace. Those people have no peace. And I knew I could have peace, and that I didn't have to earn it by going to the meetings. Another fallacy is, you do things for the dead, and that created havoc. I would lose so much time—spaces of time—when I got involved in that religion.

Jim: Do you have a way to explain that?

Paula: I seemed to have more trouble spiritually then, so that may have been when more demons came in and attached themselves. That's how I would explain it.

Jim: Sure. So you decided to exit from that religion?

Paula: I needed help getting out. My pastor was at our church then, and his counseling was very helpful. The police officer I was telling you about also helped keep things safe, and the assistant pastor helped me get out, too. There's always a danger that the leaders of that religion will sort of make you disappear.

Jim: Is that right? No wonder you needed help leaving.

Paula: They brought somebody all the way from their regional center to convince me to stay. They finally sent me a letter a year later and said I was out. I was glad to get the letter.

Jim: How long was that exit before getting into the Christian hospital unit last summer?

Paula: A year and a half.

Jim: So for a year and a half after that you still hadn't landed in the right treatment?

Paula: Right. I had been talking with my pastor. That was before he knew very much about how to approach it.

Jim: Well, once you got into the intensive therapy, the inpatient work, you said treatment was six to eight hours a day?

Paula: Right. Sometimes as long as twelve hours.

Jim: That must have been exhausting for you.

Paula: It was. I did so much work, and then I would just keel over! Some days . . . you know what would happen some days? Some days I would go in to see the psychologist at the beginning. I would start, and then it was supper time! [Laughs]

Jim: Where did the day go?

Paula: It was sort of like this. The psychologist would look terrible and so exhausted when we would walk out, and the nurse would tell him how bad he looked, and then she would ask me how come I did not look exhausted.

My answer would be, "Because I just went in!" [Practically the whole day would have passed while she was "in" an alter that her host personality did not know.]

Jim: The joke was on them! But later, when you integrated all the parts, did you gain the memory of what had happened during those blank spots?

Paula: I did, because I gained the facts of what was talked about. During those blank spots, the therapists evidently would share some things about themselves to the alters, at the start of the sessions. Those facts, like their age or where they went to school, for example, I remembered after integration, even though "I" didn't hear them the first time.

Jim: Do you also now remember the things that were done in therapy during those blank hours?

Paula: Yes, I do.

Jim: What was that like?

Paula: In a way, it is like waking up and not remembering a dream until later in the day, and then you remember the whole thing.

Jim: What kind of dreams were they?

Paula: Some of them were pretty hard. When some of the little ones were integrated I cried, because I couldn't believe that much horrible stuff could have happened to me.

Jim: One of the things I try to point my clients toward is, while they are still separate, to have the child parts receive healing before they are integrated.

Paula: That is what my psychologist had done, and that is why there was not such an *intense* reaction as normally would have happened during integration. After a memory was gone through, then Jesus would take the pain away and healing would come. The psychologist would share the memory. There would be confession of any stronghold, then any demons attached would be gotten rid of. So the integration was not so intense.

Jim: You knew the pain was bad, but you couldn't remember the bad pain itself, because you had been healed?

Paula: Yes. I knew the facts, but the feeling was *much* less—if it hadn't been, I would have run down the road screaming!

Jim: We hope that will happen for all people in therapy—that they will get the healing before the integration, so the rest of them don't have to experience the pain that the one part went through.

Paula: Of all the parts that were integrated, in only one did it seem that the healing had not taken place. That was the hardest, and I think it was the youngest memory.

Jim: About how young?

Paula: About two and a half. When I got that—I don't know what to call it—that person back to me, it was terrible. The therapists thought they would have to stop the integration, because the pain was so bad. It was as if I was back there.

Jim: It wasn't like that in the other integrations?

Paula: In the others it was like I was seeing a movie, but in that one, it was like I was just back there, and the feelings were as bad as they were originally.

Jim: Did you reseparate from that young part, in order to get healing, or did you get healing after she came in?

Paula: The therapists thought they were not going to be able to integrate her before my hospitalization ended, so they were going to leave her out. They asked me, and I said, "No. We have come too far." I was afraid. I didn't want to leave the hospital the second time, and not be finished.

Jim: When you left the hospital, were you "finished," or did you find out about more alters later?

Paula: After the first hospitalization there were some that came up later. Then when I went back the second time, the two-and-a-half-year-old integrated, and the younger ones were integrated. Now, there are still three or four, I think, that have not been completed. I did not call my psychologist because I felt it was my fault that there were a few alters left, so I was embarrassed and afraid to call. But in December I did call him and said, "I think we may have a minor difficulty." He said that at a future date we could do another hospitalization if I chose.

Jim: To what extent are the new findings upsetting your daily life?

Paula: There are short periods of time missing. I would suspect, from what I find around the house, that there is a child left, and a couple of teenagers.

Jim: You don't have direct contact with them—you just see evidence of them?

Paula: Yes, when I find toys out or I see different clothes in my closet. I say, "Hum?" but there are no massive spaces of time missing, and there has not been the cutting of my wrists, like before. I've lost none of the things I gained in the integrations so far. But I guess some more work has to be done.

Jim: Do you need to be hospitalized again, or is there a local place you could go?

Paula: No. My therapist is away right now, and is in contact with my psychologist, and is willing to learn, but he is not ready to do the integrations yet. I will probably go back for a short stay, to tie up loose ends—minor details, when compared to the past.

Jim: You know, I'm trying to have people like you describe what the integration process was like for them. People who are interested in this book might not relate to that very easily. How would you describe your integrative experiences? What was it like for you?

Paula: When a personality was integrated, it was like a moving picture, showing things that had happened, suddenly appeared before my eyes. Before integration, I had photographs of all my birth children in albums, and they didn't mean anything to me. When one alter was integrated, I suddenly remembered my daughter's *whole* childhood. All the pictures made sense then! The motion picture moved very fast. At some spots I was happy and at other spots I was crying. It was difficult when the alters who had so many bad things happen to them were integrated, because it hurt so much to see why they had been created in the first place—and what they were covering up. It was difficult, but it was still the motion picture, right in front of my eyes. It was as if I had been asleep for a long time and then woke up. Years had passed, but then it all made sense, and I knew how I got from one spot to the other. That's the best way I know to describe it.

Jim: It's almost like you're in a dark hallway, and when the integration takes place, the lights go on and you see everything.

Paula: And it's so fantastic! It's so wonderful to remember things. It was wonderful to remember so many new things about my daughter and my son—to *know!* People used to talk about what their kids did when they were this age and that age. I made things up, because I didn't know. Then after one alter was integrated, I was so excited because I could finally tell people for *real,* "I know what happened!"

Jim: That must be a joy almost inexpressible.

Paula: It is. I cried and was happy at the same time. It was like extremes of emotions. When the hard memories came, I experienced the sadness and the pain. Even though I am an adult, and it happened when I was so young, it's as though it had just now happened, and it hurt very much. Both sides.

The other part that's exciting is that little bits of things keep coming back more and more. I didn't get all the memory from each alter completely, because I don't think I could grasp it, but little bits and pieces keep coming back. Not so much now, but the first several days after we finished each one, I would see something and say, "Hey! I remember that!" Of course, I didn't say it out loud, at least not in front of people.

Jim: It still is exciting?

Paula: Yes, it is. I wouldn't trade the hours of work or the knowledge of the pain for anything, because of all the joy I have now. It was worth it. I don't understand why people have to abuse children, young people, or even their spouses, but it's been worth going through the therapy, for the joy at the end of it, even with all the pain and the crying.

Eventually, you laugh. One of my sons called this morning. I had not told my daughter, but I had told him about the MPD when I was in the hospital. Today is the first time I have talked with him since I've been out of the hospital. He said, "Mom, you sound great. You really sound great!" He said, "I'm so happy for you. I wish I could be there just to hug you!" He said, "I'm proud of you, Mom." And it's neat because he also said, "You know, Mom, I can remember some of the hard times when you'd get lost and didn't know where you were." Of course he didn't understand then why it happened that way, but he understands now and our relationship has a future.

Jim: Hope. A future. Your life is just taking off!

Paula: I can handle myself now in a crowd. The church I had been going to got a new pastor, and he wasn't what they wanted, and the church started dissolving. Before, I would just have gone along with somebody to a different church, but now I said, "Hey, I'm a person. I can decide for myself." So I chose a little church, and went there, and I liked it. I joined it, and now I play the organ in all the services and I play for the choir. I'm involved in Sunday School, and when people there ask me about my real family, I just say, "Well, they never had much to do with me." I don't have to explain everything to them.

They say, "It doesn't matter. We will be your real family."

Jim: That is what Jesus said to his disciples, who were away from their original families: "Your true family are the people who do the will of the Father in Heaven" (see Matthew 12:50). The family of God is supposed to be a person's true family. Now you have a future and a family!

Paula: A family that accepts me just the way I am!

Jim: People want to know just how all this progress came about. If you had to explain to somebody about the psychological and the spiritual parts of therapy, how would you do it?

Paula: Psychological and spiritual parts of therapy.

Jim: Was that a loaded question or what?

Paula: That's a double-barreled question!

Jim: I want you to feel free to talk about whatever God was doing for you, about whatever spiritual things were happening for you, and whatever psychological things were happening, and how they interrelate. I have written some things about this and you haven't read them, so it would be interesting for me to hear how our ideas are the same or different.

Paula: There was a great deal of depression, a great deal of fear, and a great deal of anger. The fear came from not understanding what was going on, and I didn't understand people's reactions. The anger would come when I found the furniture changed around, or new food in the kitchen instead of what I had bought, or different clothes in the closet. I felt great depression and sadness, I think, because at that time I was seeking an answer. You know the man in *Pilgrim's Progress?*

Jim: Yes.

Paula: He was constantly seeking, seeking. I think that's how I looked at it. I was constantly seeking an answer. And because of my belief in God, and my belief of salvation, I knew there had to be an answer. But people would be cruel and say, "You just don't believe enough. You don't pray enough. You don't do this or that enough. God will heal you, probably when you get to heaven, but God will take care of it. Don't worry about it." They really did not know what was going on.

Jim: So what you were getting from the religious community was mostly guilt that you weren't good enough, and that's why God wasn't healing you?

Paula: Right. Guilt trip. Or there must be something wrong. "You haven't really forgiven someone"; or, "You must have done some awful sin or this wouldn't be happening to you."

Jim: The blame kept coming back on you?

Paula: I was always told it was all my fault.

Jim: So how does a person overcome something like that?

Paula: One way is to build walls against people. You do what you have to do to fulfill your obligations, but you just stay away from people. After a while you don't reach out any more. I think I quit reaching out to people a long time ago, until people started reaching out to me at my church. My former lady therapist also reached out to me and became a friend.

Jim: Was there some kind of a spiritual component in your therapy? Why don't you talk about that for a minute.

Paula: The spiritual side now you mean? Like in the integration?

Jim: Anywhere that you saw God active, or any spiritual forces that were helping you.

Paula: I was split into five thousand pieces, you know. To me, each one was like a person, so each one had its own spiritual life. Before I could be integrated, my psychologist worked with each alter, so that particular one could accept Christ as personal savior. That way each part would have the Holy Spirit within, and they would all work together.

And I had to forgive people. I had to forgive God, because I had blamed God: "Why did You do this? Why did You let those people do this to me?" First I had to confess my sin of hating those who abused me, then thank God for forgiving us for hating Him. And then I had to forgive myself for hating me before I could even begin working. I had to get myself right spiritually before I was ready to be able to do anything. I hated how I was. I hated the fact that I couldn't fix me. If I was so smart and so intelligent, why couldn't I fix it?

Jim: Can you imagine going through this without God?

Paula: I don't think I could have. I don't think you can get healing if you don't believe in God. Jehovah Rapha—the God who heals. If you have a prayer life, you have God's forgiveness and salvation, so you can accept His healing. If I didn't have God, I would go out and kill these people for what they did to me, even though it was a long time ago. I would go out and kill every one of them.

I don't think I ever would have become a whole person without God healing the memories. I don't think I ever would have become integrated, because if the memories aren't healed, I don't think there can be a solid integration. It would be only temporary. And without God getting rid of the evil spirits and the demons that are attached, things would get worse.

I told my pastor when I first saw him, "If you are only going to do surface work, or if you are only fascinated because this is something new, leave me alone. I will be in worse condition than I was when I came in the door." I think that is what would happen to people who try to integrate without God. It would make things worse. There would be more fragmentation, and I think evil spirits could attack because of the fragmentation. That's my opinion.

Jim: Well, I must wholeheartedly agree with you, right down the line. If there isn't healing, the integration is going to be very short-lived.

Paula: And no one else can give healing but God. Who else can heal? You can talk to therapists until you are blue in the face! I talked to a lot of therapists who didn't know what they were talking about. You can be analyzed, psychoanalyzed, therapized, and everything else, but if there's no healing by God, there's no one to hold you. No one who *really* knows you. No one who can heal you.

Jim: Well, you sure went through the therapy lickety-split. What did it take, about four months?

Paula: Yes.

Jim: For all that integrative work?

Paula: My therapist said it would have taken us about three to five years to have done that much at an hour or two a week in therapy.

Jim: That's pretty impressive.

Paula: We worked hard. My psychologist said he didn't know if anyone else could go through it that fast. He said it would depend on their relationship with Jesus, their faith in God, their Bible background, and their spiritual walk.

Jim: From what I have been able to tell, the amount of faith you have as you come into it either sets you way ahead or you find you are starting from square one.

Paula: Right.

Jim: And if you have to start from square one with all of your personalities each needing to get to know God from the start, it takes a lot longer.

Paula: Right.

Jim: If you already had God active inside most of your personalities, or if some of your personalities had a strong faith, it probably would spread. It would be like gaining momentum.

Paula: Right. Like they were teaching the other ones.

Jim: So evangelizing was going on inside you?

Paula: After the first hospitalization, I came home for a while, and when I went back my psychologist mentioned that one of the alters he had talked with had been teaching the others about Christ.

Jim: And you didn't even know about it?

Paula: That's right.

Jim: Was that pretty effective?

Paula: Yes.

Jim: At what point, then, did you become aware of demonic activity?

Paula: I knew it was there a long time ago.

Jim: Was that something you hoped you wouldn't ever have to face?

Paula: Right.

Jim: And how did you finally decide that you needed to face it, and declare spiritual warfare?

Paula: When I went to see my pastor for the very first session, that was why I went to see him. The police officer knew that he worked with people who were demon possessed, and the police officer felt I was demon possessed.

Jim: You were hoping you could just kick out the demons, and you would be all finished?

Paula: Right. I was hoping, "That's it!" When I went to see him the first time, it was a long session, with a lot of getting rid of evil spirits, and I felt great. I thought, "This is good. I'm doing great. This is fine." Then I was supposed to go back the next week. In the meantime, my furniture moved, my clothes left, and toys were all over the place. So I went back about five different times, frustrated because "there's no answer." The pastor would get rid of some evil spirits, and then it seemed like I would always be worse in a short time. I think Luke 11:26 applies here, and until the alters had their healing and were integrated, I don't think there would have been release from the demon activity. Without this process, I feel it leaves a weak point for demons to come in. It leaves an open door.

Jim: That is right. Well, yours is an uplifting story. Do you have some other things you'd like to say?

Paula: Yes. Sometimes I would get angry because all those toys were in my house, and I would give them away. Within a week, or even a day sometimes, I'd come back, and my closets would be full of toys again.

Jim: Have you figured out what happened?

Paula: Now I know, because some of the alters were little, and they never had some of these toys. And so they confiscated them!

Jim: But after you were all integrated, did those blank spots get filled in?

Paula: Yes, but I feel sorry for the people who lived around me during all that confusion—how could they begin to understand?

Jim: Well, it sounds like you have a real peace about the therapy that you have done.

Paula: Yes.

Jim: How do you plan to go on from here? Do you have a direction in your life?

Paula: Well, one thing I have to do is learn some new coping skills, so I don't have to fragment because of fear. But now, all of a sudden, I have *too much* time!

Jim: It's not disappearing as much any more?

Paula: That's right. What do I do now? I think I want to learn to be more constructive with my time, you know, planning time and doing things. I would like to write. I would like to write what's happened all the way from beginning to end. I don't know if anything would ever happen with it, but I would just like to write it for myself.

Jim: That would be fascinating, and it would help you, too. I think it would cement your progress in place.

Paula: Right. *Cement* is a good word. In my mind I picture that this book has all of my life right there—the ending of my fragmented period, and a new beginning.

Jim: That chapter of your life is over, isn't it?

Paula: Yes.

Jim: There were fragments and disagreements within you, and now that you are a whole individual, you can start a new chapter.

Paula: And I can be a real person. A whole person. And I'm a grandmother! Isn't that funny? You know that sounds silly, but I never pictured myself as a grandmother, in all this time. You know, it didn't *fit* any place in me. I was at the birth of one of my grandsons, but I didn't remember it! I was *told* I was there, and one of the integrations put me through the whole birth process, and I saw my grandson delivered! That was so exciting!

Also, I think I'll try going back to school. I got my associate degree two years ago, and I may go for my bachelor's and my master's. I can do it now. I'm free. I'm whole.

Jim: Do you feel that, since you have so much more time on your hands, you will do better in school? You will study better? Focus better?

Paula: I think so. I had a 3.75 grade average.

Jim: You can't get much better than that!

Paula: When I got my associate degree, I didn't even know if I did it! [This particular personality did not know then because amnesic alters unknown to her were the ones who had attended the school, and when she got the degree, those class-attending alters were not the ones who picked up the diploma.]

Another thing has happened: I have found out I can draw, and I also play the piano very well.

Jim: Really? You mean part of you knew how to play the piano, and the rest of you didn't know? It was kind of a surprise—"Oh, by the way, I play the piano!"?

Paula: Yes, and I can write well, too. Several things have come up that I can do very well. It's like, "Hey, this is great!" [Both have a good laugh.]

Jim: What a joy. What do you like to draw?

Paula: I have been drawing a lot of flowers—feminine-type things. Most of my life I have been masculinely dressed, because having been severely abused by men, I hated them. I felt that if I was a male, I would not be abused, but it's different now. I went to the beauty shop. Can you imagine *me* going to the beauty shop and *liking* it?

Jim: Most of your life you have been more masculine?

Paula: Uh-huh. Many of the alters were men, but when the healing took place, they became female. They all took on female names before integration.

Jim: And that's taken a shift lately?

Paula: Yes. When I came back from the hospital this time, people said, "You look so different, Paula. Your hair is so different." They say even my hair color is different, but it's not. To me it doesn't look any different, and I don't use anything on it.

And people said, "You walk different. What's happened, anyway?"

But I don't have to tell my story to everyone. It's not everyone's business. I say, "Oh, I guess they did me a lot of good at the hospital!"

Jim: So you are afraid to tell about the MPD?

Paula: I don't want people to ridicule it, or try to punch holes in the healing. The people who accept it, who are my friends, I have talked to about it. I have talked to my sons about it, but I have not made it common knowledge.

Jim: That sounds wise. Have you picked up on any kind of subtle, but nonetheless evident, bias against MPD?

Paula: Oh, yes! Shortly after they diagnosed the MPD, remember, I was in the car wreck, and I was raped by one of the paramedics. That was vicious. It was taken to court, and they changed the district attorney twice on it, because of the MPD diagnosis. At the secular counseling center here, they did not want to take it to court, because they were afraid that if it were brought out that I had MPD, it would cause more problems for me publicly. It had already created problems in my therapy. And after going to court many times, they dropped my case. The judge did not want anybody with MPD in his courtroom.

Jim: I can hardly believe my ears! Did you just say that a judge didn't want someone with MPD in his courtroom?

Paula: Yes.

Jim: That's almost unlawful, isn't it?

Paula: Well, the district attorney fought it, and there was some kind of political stuff. It even went to the state supreme court twice because of that. Like I said, it's a small town, and the case was dropped. The rapist was told to leave the state. He had raped two other women, who were fixing to come forward, too, but first they had to get me into the courtroom. Finally the judge let me in the courtroom one day, for five minutes. We had been waiting for this for over two years.

Jim: And then it lasted five minutes, and that was the end?

Paula: That was the end.

Jim: And it all came to nothing, because he didn't want MPD in the courtroom?

Paula: Right.

Jim: So there you were, hoping for two years that you would get some justice, and in five minutes it was all thrown out the window!

Paula: We never got past the preliminaries. We never did. I got dressed a million times to go into that courtroom, and waited in the district attorney's office for hours and hours, but the judge wouldn't come out. So there's a stigma attached to it—that's why I don't go around talking about it.

I know I'm different now. I know God has healed me. I know God is helping me to grow and learn new ways to cope with the excitement of life, and to deal with the sadness of life too, all without dissociation. It may take some time for me to do well at it, but I'm not going to advertise what's going on. I am not willing to booby-trap it.

Jim: Well, I have always held that safety is top priority.

Paula: That's it.

Jim: And I think you deserve a little safety, after being raped and thrown out of court, like an old piece of trash. I hope some day our society will find a place for you in its trophy case, instead of its waste basket.

Paula: Thank you. I prayed this morning before I called you, and I prayed all day, because my hope is that this will help others know that there is help out there, that help can be found, and that you are not some riddle, just because you have MPD. You can be a whole person, and God loves you even before you become a whole person. God loves you when you are all in pieces.

10

RICK HAMMOND: Spiritual Warfare

PART I. Demonic Entanglement and Release

RICK* wrote me a letter after he read my first book. He wanted to get to know me, compare a few notes, and talk with me about spreading the word that both the spiritual *and* the psychological aspects of treatment are vital. He told me a few things about his therapy, his family and his background, and it seemed a chapter in this book would be a good place to let him tell his story.

His call came at just the right time for me. I was wanting to talk to someone who had already completed therapy in order to put my ideas to a test: Do the spiritual and psychological things I observed contradict other people's experiences?

It was a little risky for me, as I prepared to dialogue with Rick, knowing that there could be a clash of spiritual world views, and I couldn't help feeling like a beginner. Rick had a lot of poise, and a quiet sense of confidence that the Lord had done some remarkable things in his life. I could hardly wait to find out about them.

---

*   Rick and his therapist, Tom Hawkins, do not want their correct names withheld. They are open about all of this, and can be contacted through the publishers for verification or for further information.

He had been a pastor for twenty-five years, and only during the last two years had he known just what his condition was—"a demonized multiple." Rick sent me a fairly long autobiographical manuscript, and I was struck with how well he writes. He had been through a series of morbid childhood experiences with death, and with honoring the dead, which was a part of his demonic entanglement. He also sent me an audio tape of one of his therapy sessions, which included working with different alters, and some exorcism. The tape illustrates how to discover the difference between alters and demons, and how the spiritual and the psychological components of therapy are intertwined. I thought the tape was important enough that I asked Rick to let me transcribe parts of it for this chapter, and he agreed wholeheartedly. So did his therapist.

I know that when evil spirits are cast out in the name of Jesus they must leave. So why do "they" sometimes stay? They may be personalities, and therefore cannot be "cast out." Or they may not leave because the person, or even one alter, may have "given ground" to the spirit at some point. Perhaps a vow was made, or there was a decision, an act of the alter's will, to allow the evil spirit's presence. In such a case, it is necessary for the person to renounce the vow or the decision, from all his or her parts, in order to take away the evil spirit's ground. When a spirit is attached in this way, there can be some self-destructive and life-threatening consequences, and the person's life will change dramatically after the spirit leaves. This tape shows not only how dastardly the spirits can be, but also how, intent on destruction, they can use a person's will to hold their ground. Here are excerpts from a telephone conversation, and from the exorcism session.

Jim: Tell me, how did you get interested in talking with me about your background and recovery, and your direction in life?

Rick: I guess it was two or three months ago, I pulled you into the process when I was moving toward integration. We came across a manuscript of your book. It was a manuscript you presented to somebody I know. [That was before the book went into print.]. I was curious about your manuscript, but I had deliberately withheld myself from any literature on the subject at all—the demonic activity, or the MPD aspects. I hadn't exposed myself to any of that literature because I was so concerned, early on, with being led along the right path.

Jim: You mean you wanted to avoid any kind of so-called suggestibility?

Rick: Right. I didn't want there to be any possibility that I would start following along any particular line. I felt extremely vulnerable. So your manuscript came across my desk, and I passed it around, and my wife and our children read it. Eric, our son, was discussing some of the passages in it that related to the young woman named Beth. The way she expressed some of her experiences made me realize they were similar to mine. So I was quite interested in that. I think that's the only passage of the book I read at the time.

Then as we moved on toward integration I was particularly interested in going back and reading some of the literature. At that point I started looking at your book.

Jim: You mean you had no knowledge of what was in the book during most of your therapy?

Rick: That's right. I wanted to see how my experiences matched up with what you were writing about generally, and then with some specific people in the book.

Jim: Did you find our material compatible?

Rick: That's when I became intrigued, because I found your approach, and even the vocabulary you used, to be very similar to things that I experienced. That served as a confirmation for me. We used the same methodology.

Then my wife and I went to Chicago. This was our second meeting with Dr. Dickason. We had been in his office about five minutes when he opened his briefcase and pulled out your book, and asked if we had looked at it or read it. At that time my wife had but I hadn't. He began reading some passages out of it to us, comparing our experiences with what you had written. He was very positive about your book, by the way—he has had a great deal of experience with the demonic element of all of this.

Jim: Fred Dickason?

Rick: Yes. We chatted in his office about that and about demonic experience. It was a strong confirmation.

Jim: Well, it came at just the right time. I was trying to conceptualize this present book. People like you provide exactly the kind of information I'm looking for, and that is to discover if God works in the same way all over the globe. If He is doing certain things here in California, it would make sense to me that He would do the same things there in Texas. So it's a confirmation to me, too, for you to say our experiences match.

Rick: And they did all the way along, from the very beginning, in dealing with some of the general issues regarding MPD, and in the diagnosis and strategy you have been using. But it wasn't only that certain things were similar. It was the whole pattern. You would have to know me better to know how important it was for me to know that what I was experiencing was not unique. It has confirmed for me the reliability of the process I have been through.

Jim: That's a work of grace for us all, and I'm pleased with that. Can you say a little bit about what it was like to dissociate and integrate? I know that's one of the things you have gone through, and most people don't understand it.

Rick: I have been dissociating for more than forty years. I'm 47 now, and did not become aware of it—the word *dissociation* didn't become part of my vocabulary until about a year and a half ago. I have been dissociating for a long while, and I had developed a whole vocabulary to explain those behaviors from just being "moody" to being "sentimental." I'd say the closest I ever got to psychological language was "burnout." I was forced to find explanations and vocabulary to explain behavior I didn't understand. As I had got older, into my 30s and 40s, certain critical periods in my life had drawn me to therapists, but usually, after two or three sessions, a particular crisis would have passed and I would float back to the explanation most acceptable to me. Usually, I was "overworked." I took all the psychological tests, so I was pretty sure I wasn't crazy, but I knew something was desperately wrong, and I knew it was more than just mood shifts.

Jim: And all this time you were a pastor?

Rick: I have been a pastor for about twenty-five years.

Jim: Twenty-five years of going with what seemed like moodiness or depression, and something was wrong but you were not sure what, and yet you were able to do God's work?

Rick: Most of the time. Have you listened to the tape of the exorcism session that I sent you?

Jim: Yes.

Rick: One of the specific vows I took as a child, during the abuse period, was to never cooperate and to always mess things up when they were going well. The tape explains how that started. It was a definite cycle in my life. The original cycles of probably five or six years were healed within this year. Things would be going well in the pastorate, for example, or in graduate school, or in relationships, or life in general, and I would almost deliberately create a crisis, a situation which would bring that period of relative tranquility to an end. But I would pass through that crisis. Sometimes it would last a matter of days, sometimes as much as six months, and then I'd begin the process all over again.

Jim: Well, how much of this would you say was a spiritual point of conflict versus a psychological point of conflict, if you can make a distinction?

Rick: There was definitely demonic activity, but I wasn't aware of that. My entire theological model disallowed that possibility. I was led to believe that demonic activity was foreign to the experience of any Christian, other than just the general satanic activity we were all exposed to. That would all be external. So, even in the worst of times, I never remotely considered the possibility of any demonic activity. As I look back now, I see that there was. We uncovered, through the process of therapy, some specific promises and vows I had made (during times of torture), with regard to receptivity to demons. For several years, the spiritual issue for me was never being able to find an answer to what was going on with me.

Jim: The demonic influence was masking and confusing?

Rick: It was masking. It was confusing. I felt I was being seized. I would do all the right things and use all the appropriate spiritual weapons, but it wouldn't come up against a depression. It wouldn't come up against the self-destructive tendencies I had at those periods of time. Nothing worked. So the spiritual ramification was to create serious doubts in my faith. For some reason, I believed I was excluded from grace.

Jim: You were excluded from grace because of the vows you had made as a youngster?

Rick: Yes, but I wasn't aware of them. All I knew was that I was in desperate difficulty a great deal of the time. I thought that if a Christian were walking in Christ, things like depression were not part of us.

Jim: I think this would be a good time to review parts of the exorcism tape you sent me. It will illustrate how the spiritual and the psychological were toxically intertwined in your life—they were killing each other.

* * *

DEMONIC ENTANGLEMENT

The tape begins during a session in which Tom, the pastoral counselor, is trying to induce cooperation between Rick's personalities. Philip, Shelby, Jason, David, Byron and Mr. Macquet are alters in Rick's system who take turns working with Tom in this session.

Tom: Philip, you step aside and let me talk to Shelby. Shelby, I'm your friend, and I'm here to help you.

Shelby: (Whispering very softly.) I know.

Tom: Is my guess right, that Philip's got some spirits?

Shelby: (Almost inaudible.) Yes.

Tom: Uh-huh; I figured so from the way he was acting.

(New voice): Shut up, Shelby!

Tom: Listen, Philip . . .

Philip: Shut up, Shelby! (He speaks in an emotionless tone.)

Tom: Uh, maybe you've forgotten. You saw the 225 spirits leave, didn't you?

Shelby: Yes.

Philip: Shut up, Shelby!

Tom: Jesus' power is greater. Do you know anybody who can tell us about the alters on the deeper layer?

(Heavy sigh.)

Tom: That's okay. Jesus will keep you safe, Shelby.

Shelby: (Whispering.) They will get in so much trouble.

Tom: Who will get in so much trouble?

Shelby: David.

Tom: Is he the one who knows so much about this? (Inaudible whisper from Shelby.) Oh, Philip *makes* him do those things he did.

Shelby: (Still whispering.) David is the opposite from Philip. David is good, too. Can't talk!

Tom: Uh-huh. I think, Shelby, that we need to ask God for wisdom, because we need to know what to do.

Philip: Shut up. I don't like you. I don't have to talk to you.

Tom: No, but David wants me to talk to you, Philip.

Philip: I don't like you, and I don't have to talk to you.

Tom: You know, Philip, Jesus is the one who has the power to save you from the evil spirits.

Philip: That's a lie.

Tom: Jesus sent away the 225 spirits, didn't he?

Shelby: (Whispering.) Forty-six.

Tom: Can you tell me about that?

Shelby: He was supposed to die when he was 46. Because David was so good.

Philip: Shut up! Shut up!

Tom: [Tom came to a conclusion about Philip at this point.] Philip, your game is uncovered. You're not a part of Rick at all, are you?

"Philip": Shut up!

Tom: In the name of Jesus Christ (interrupted by another "Shut up!") tell me what right ("Shut up!") you have to be ("Shut up!") in Rick. ("Shut up!")

Tom: Listen, I have the authority of Jesus Christ . . . (Loud noises.)

"Philip": Shut up! Shut up! Shut up! [Every word uttered by "Philip" is still said in exactly the same emotionless tone. It could have been spoken by a robot.]

Tom: "Philip," in the name of Jesus Christ, tell me your real name. You are using the name "Philip" to fake us out, aren't you? What's your real name?

(A sinister snicker breaks out, in a completely different voice from "Philip's," with a jeering quality, and lots of emotional inflection. "Philip," the spirit, has given up his attempt to sound like an alter.)

Unidentified voice: I hate you! I hate you!

Tom: I know now why you hate me. ("I hate you!" keeps repeating.) In the name of Jesus Christ, tell me who you are. What is your real name?

The jeering voice: I have a right to be here.

Tom: Okay, in the name of Jesus, tell me what your right is.

The jeering voice: They didn't kill him.

Tom: He took a vow that he would die at age 46. Is that right?

(The eerie snickering breaks out again, louder than before, and keeps going for about twenty seconds.)

Tom: (Still calm, he starts to talk despite the snickering.) I'm not impressed by your laughter. You're serving the losing side.

The jeering voice: (Sounds a little like "Philip," but now speaks with abundant emotional inflection.) I hate you!

Tom: You're going to have to leave. You know that. I want to talk to Rick. ("I hate you!" keeps repeating.) Rick, push your way out. Philip is losing his power over you, Rick. Philip, you step aside.

(Heavy sighing, and Rick has trouble breathing.)

Tom: Rick, are you here? (Gasping is heard.) Father, in the name of Jesus Christ, I pray that You would set Rick free from whatever is keeping him from breathing. (Gasping continues.) Father, help him to realize this is a painful memory, but it is in the past now, and he can be freed from it. (Gasping is becoming quieter, but continues.) Father, I pray You would send an angel to minister to Rick, and show him that You can set him free. You kept him alive then, and You can keep him alive now.

(Gasping takes on a whimpering quality.) I know this is painful, Rick, but you survived it the first time, and by God's grace you can survive the memory tonight. As soon as you can, please tell me what happened next.

(Groaning continues, and after about thirty seconds, an unidentified voice softly speaks.) Rick said to lie still. "Sing songs in your head. Play the piano in your head. Don't move! Don't move!"

Tom: What happened next? ("Don't move!" continues.) You laid still for a long time. What happened next?

Unidentified voice: (Groaning.) It's dirt. Take the dirt off your eyes. You can look up and you can see them laughing!

Tom: That must have been terrifying.

Unidentified voice: (Moaning subsides.) You breathe and the dirt goes in your mouth and in your nose. David says, "Sing songs in your head." They all go to the bathroom on you. (Groaning starts again.) They pull you out.

Tom: You must have been really scared.

Another unidentified voice: (In a lower register.) They never want to see David again. David is good. They want to bury him. Jason knows.

Tom: David, did you tell me about the burial? ("Yes.") Well, David, I'm real sorry for what happened to you.

David: I'm dead! (Repeats that while Tom talks.)

Tom: You were sure they were going to kill you, weren't you? They buried you, saying you were no good, and they didn't want to see you any more. They didn't like you because you tried to be good. (David is now sobbing.) I'm sorry they did that to you, David, that was awful.

David: They did it many times.

Tom: I'm sorry they did that. Here's a tissue.

Lower voice: David is dead.

Tom: They wanted you to think you were dead, but you're alive—you're talking to me. You told me what happened, and you're thinking. You feel like David, don't you? They buried you but they didn't kill you, David. Since you can play the piano, that means you are alive, doesn't it?

David: Will they try to kill me again?

Tom: They tried to kill you so Jason would make a deal, that at 46 Rick would die. That's why everything has been coming apart this year. Rick was 46 this year, wasn't he?

(*"Philip"* interrupts for three full minutes. He talks about hating Tom, and refuses to let any alters talk. Then, just after Tom tells him to step aside in the name of Jesus Christ, the moaning begins again.)

Tom: I'm sorry they did that to you, Rick. They tortured both you and David. (Deriding laughter.) Step aside, "Philip"! David [Tom recognized that David had momentarily switched in and was reliving a traumatic episode.], you can breathe now. Breathe slowly. That's a memory. It's a real memory, but it's past. Try to get in touch with the present. [Then Tom realized Rick had switched back in.] Just slow down your breathing, Rick.

Rick, you're not going to have any peace until we get rid of "Philip," and he doesn't want to go. But you know he's a spirit, don't you?

You want to get rid of "Philip," don't you? (Tapping sounds start—Rick's hand hitting his head, and face, under direction of the spirit. He had to be restrained repeatedly.) "Philip," step aside. Jason, I need to talk to you. Jason, are you here? Have you been listening to what's going on? Can you tell me about the vow? What was the deal?

Jason: I told God I was sorry. [In previous sessions, Jason had renounced the many times he had made "deals" with spirits, but had not recalled this specific vow.]

Tom: I know. But we need to get rid of "Philip."

Jason: Four.

Tom: There are four spirits?

Jason: Yes.

Tom: Do you think "Philip" is one of them?

Jason: Yes. I'm sorry. I'm sorry! God said He forgave me!

Tom: Yes, but you need to get rid of the spirits.

Jason: Forty-six. Forty-six. I would die. I would die.

Tom: What else did you promise?

Jason: Never cooperate. Never cooperate.

Tom: With whom?

Jason: Never cooperate with Rick.

Tom: And you got other alters to help you with that plan? What else was in the vow?

Jason: When things were going well, do something that would mess everything up. (Crying.) I'm sorry. I'm sorry!

Tom: God forgives you, Jason. It's okay. It's all over now. It's not going to happen any more. As far as you know, four spirits came in then, when you made that vow?

Jason: One for each part. One for each part of the vow, and "Philip" to oversee it and be in charge.

Tom: Okay, Jason, are you ready to renounce the vow? Can you say, "I don't want Rick to die at 46; I renounce the vow not to cooperate, and I renounce the vow that when things are going well, I'll mess it up"?

(Jason says that. Some panting is heard, and continues.)

Tom: "Philip," step aside. "Philip," step aside.

Jason: I renounce the vow. I renounce the vow.

Tom: Say, "I renounce 'Philip' and the other three spirits." (Tapping sounds, which is spirit-induced self-hitting.) "Philip," step aside. Step aside. (Moaning and shortness of breath.) Are you ready to renounce those spirits?

Jason: Yes.

Tom: Father, in the name of Jesus Christ, help Jason to talk. Set Jason free, so he can make this renunciation. Jason, I know you feel bad, but God has forgiven you, so let's get rid of these spirits. (The struggling sounds increase—moaning and difficult breathing.) Jason, stay here. "Philip," step aside. Jason, stay here, stay with me. (Crying is heard.) Jason, are you still here? Jason, stay with me. Father, set Jason free, I pray. Help us to have wisdom to deal with all of these personalities, and their traumas. (Moaning continues.) Father, loose his tongue, so he can renounce. Say, "I, Jason, renounce the vows."

Jason: I, Jason, renounce the vows.

Tom: "I renounce 'Philip' and the other three spirits."

Jason: (Voice getting stronger.) I renounce "Philip" and the other three spirits.

Tom: That's right. "I'm covered by the shed blood of Jesus."

Jason: I'm covered by the shed blood of Jesus.

Tom: "And in Jesus' name, I command you to leave."

Jason: And in Jesus' name, I command you to leave.

(David also renounces the vows, and says he has come over to God's side.)

David: I'm alive! I'm alive!

Tom: God kept you alive.

David: I'm not sure. (That is repeated while Tom talks.)

Tom: David, when you get rid of these spirits, you'll feel alive again. Father, I pray You would help David to feel alive, so he can make this renunciation. Father, help him to see that then is not now. He's survived the grave experience—being covered up and the burial. He's alive now. I pray You'd help him to see that.

David: I'm not sure. ("I'm alive!" changed to "I'm not sure." This resulted from continuing spiritual harassment.)

Tom: David, can you feel this finger? Do you know dead people can't feel? ("Yes.") We can make the spirits go away. As I understand it, the first part of the vow is that Rick will die at 46. Are you ready to renounce that?

David: I think I'm already dead.

Tom: That's a problem. If they make you think you're already dead, then you can't stop from dying. But you can feel my finger, can't you?

David: Grandma died. Anna was there, and took me into the mortuary. She said, "Look in there," when they were putting the make-up on Grandma. "That's you. That's what you look like." Every time Rick has to do a funeral now, he sees himself as dead.

Tom: That must have been awful all these years. It's been hard, hasn't it, because you thought you were dead.

David: Every time Rick goes to a funeral, at the graveyard, he has this overwhelming desire to jump into the grave. It's almost overpowering.

Tom: David, do you want to be free of that vow?

David: I'm dead.

Tom: You're alive, David. They lied to you.

David: I don't think so.

Tom: You want to ask God to make you alive?

David: But God is mad at me.

Tom: Why do you think God is mad at you? Because you asked for those spirits? (Nods, "Yes.") Okay, the Bible says, "If we confess our sins, He is faithful and just to forgive us our sins, and to cleanse us from all unrighteousness." That means He'll forgive you for every wrong thing you did. (Sneering laugh.) "Philip," step aside. Step aside, spirit. I don't want to talk with you. David, come back. "Philip" doesn't want you to do this, does he? (Whimpering.) Stay with me, David. You want to be free, and this is the way to stay alive.

David: I don't want Rick to die at 46.

Oppositional voice: I do. *I* do. *I* do. I want him to die at 46. (Repeats that fourteen times, while Tom talks.)

Tom: Spirit, step out of the way. David, come back. Father, in the name of Jesus Christ, remove this spirit. Are you here? (Nods, "Yes.") Okay. You don't want Rick to die at 46. Do you agree that you want to cooperate with Rick now, David? Can you say, "I renounce the vow not to cooperate with Rick"?

David: I renounce the vow not to cooperate with Rick.

Tom: "I renounce the vow that when things are going well, I'll mess things up."

David: I renounce the vow that when things are going well, I'll mess things up.

Tom: And, "I renounce the vow that I wanted 'Philip' and the other three under him."

David: I renounce the vow that I wanted "Philip" and the other three under him.

Tom: That's right. Good job, David. I'm going to talk with you later, but right now we need to get rid of "Philip." I want to talk with Byron. Byron, are you here?

Byron: Yeah.

Tom: Byron, I know it's been tough. I didn't know "Philip" was a spirit until just a few minutes ago. Have you been listening to what's been happening? (Nods, "Yes.") Okay, are you ready to renounce these vows?

(Byron renounces the vows. "Philip" tries to interrupt briefly only once. Another alter, Mr. Macquet, renounces the vows, too. Mr. Macquet says he knows of a spirit who pretends to be an alter.)

Tom: Do you know who that alter is?

Mr. Macquet: His name is Philip, too. You have to be careful when you call "Philip," because one lies.

Tom: How do you think I'll be able to get to the real Philip?

Mr. Macquet: I don't know. He's very clever. The spirit writes with his right hand. Make him write. When you don't know who you're talking to, make him write.

Tom: Very good. Right now I want to talk to the alter named Philip. I don't want to talk to the spirit. Philip, I want you to write for me. Write your name, Philip. (Writes with his right hand.) You're a liar. Step aside. Philip, who is part of Rick, would you come out? Would you write your name, please, Philip? (Starts writing with his left hand.) [Throughout the following interchange, the pen was shifted between the left and right hand. Apparently, God had blocked the spirit's hearing, so it was unaware the therapist knew that the alter Philip was left handed but that "Philip" the spirit was right handed.]. Good, Philip, you know how to make a *P*. Philip, this spirit's been giving you a hassle, hasn't he? He's really been scaring everybody inside. He's been out a lot, pretending to be you. I know about the vows. Jason has renounced them, Byron has renounced, Mr. Macquet has renounced, and David has renounced. So there's only one left, Philip, and that's you. Would you like to be free of these spirits? Have you come over to God's side, Philip? (He nods, "Yes.") All right.

("Philip" the spirit's voice is heard, renouncing the vow.)

Tom: Step aside, spirit. I don't want to talk to you. (The sighing that is characteristic of Philip the alter is heard.)

Philip: (Softer voice than "Philip" the spirit.) I don't want Rick to die at age 46. (He renounces the vows, and says he wants to get rid of the spirits. Then the spirit "Philip's" voice comes in again.)

Tom: Step aside. You're not Philip. Tell me what your real name is. ("I'm 'Philip.'" is repeated continuously while Tom keeps telling it to step aside.) You say your name is Philip, but that is just a name you are using to fool us. Go away and let me talk to the real Philip. Philip, these four spirits have plans for David to shoot himself in the head. So what good will it do to keep these four spirits? ("Philip" the spirit is again heard.)

Tom: Go away, spirit. You're a liar. In the name of Jesus Christ, I command you to go away, you who call yourself "Philip." Step aside.

"Philip" the spirit: I have a better name than Philip.

Tom: All right, then tell me what it is.

(After a pause, Jason emerges and talks about needing to be angry at perpetrators. He stalls the process of getting rid of the spirits, by trying to deal with the anger issue. Mr. Macquet reasons with him.)

Mr. Macquet: Jason, listen to me. You respect me, don't you? I had to realize that as smart as I am, I'm not smart enough to handle this by myself. You must listen. You are not going to be able to handle this by yourself. They are going to destroy you. Tom wants to help you. He cares about you. He's on God's side. You can trust him. You have to let go of the anger.

Tom: You see, each one of you—Byron, Mr. Macquet, Philip, and David—have legitimate issues that need to be dealt with. I'm sorry that those bad things happened, and I'm willing to help you deal with them, but we've got to take care of these spirits first. The spirits are destroying you.

"Philip" the spirit: I hate you. I hate you. I hate you.

Tom: I don't care. Your fight is with Jesus.

"Philip" the spirit: I hate you, Jesus. I hate you, Jesus.

Tom: Your place is the pit, and you know it. Step aside.

"Philip" the spirit: I will help you get a gun, and all the pain will be gone.

Tom: The alter Philip, I want to talk to you. (Incessant talking in the background—the spirit is trying to convince Rick to kill himself.) Spirit, step aside. (Groaning.) Philip, I know you are in misery, but this spirit is going to kill you all. Are you willing to give up the anger you feel over this matter? Say, "I renounce Satan's foothold." This thing is bigger than all of us. We've got to have God's power. Philip, are you willing to give up Satan's foothold?

Philip: I don't think so.

Tom: You heard Mr. Macquet and Byron and Jason. The spirits will destroy you.

"Philip" the spirit: (Voice is a little different from Philip, the alter.) I renounce the foothold.

Tom: Will you please write your name for me? (The pen is picked up with the right hand.)

(The spirit writes "Theta.") That's my name. That's my name! That's a much better name than Philip. That's my name.

[Rick had said that the Greek letter for God is "Theta." This became a real problem for Rick during much of his adult life. He studied the Greek language, and every time he saw that word *Theta,* it triggered an emotional response in him, and he unexpectedly became terribly upset.]

Tom: Okay, Theta. Your days are numbered. In the name of Jesus Christ, Theta, I command you to step aside.

Theta: I'm the top of the stairs.

Tom: You don't have nearly the power that Jesus Christ has.

Theta: We'll see.

Tom: That's exactly right. In the name of Jesus Christ I command you to step aside. You consider yourself the top of the stairs—the bright and shining one, and everybody pays attention to you, is that correct? And what are the names of the three under you, Theta?

Theta: (Sinister laughter.) Nothings!

Tom: Each of those three are "nothings"? (Sinister laughing continues.) You don't like them, do you?

Theta: They're nothings.

Tom: Theta, I command you in the name of Jesus Christ to step aside. I want to talk to the real Philip. Move aside, Theta.

Theta: Praise be to Theta. Praise be to Theta.

Tom: Philip, I want to talk to you. (Sighing is heard.) Are you back? Do you see the power Theta has?

Philip: I renounce my right to mess things up when things are going good for Rick.

Tom: Do you know of anything else you need to give up, anything that could keep the spirits there?

(Head shakes, "No.")

Tom: Then why don't you say, "I renounce the vow I took to get Theta and the three spirits under him."

Philip: They'll hurt me.

Tom: No they won't, because God will protect you, Philip.

Philip: They will really hurt me bad.

Tom: They are trying to scare you because you're their last foothold here. You don't feel very strong, do you, Philip? But you could command Theta and the three other spirits to leave in the name of Jesus Christ, and they would have to go. Now, I need to get Rick back, and you can all command the spirits to leave.

Philip: Theta has been so mad this week. I'm just really sorry. I don't know what to do.

Tom: Renounce Theta and the three under him. Say, "God, I love You, and I renounce Theta and the three spirits under him, and any other ties I have to any other spirits." (Philip says that.) Okay, very good, Philip. Now you hang in there, while I talk to

Rick. Rick, you're the last one who needs to do this. Have you been listening? (Groaning.) Theta, I don't want to talk to you.

Theta: Bang! Bang! Bang! (Repeats this softly.)

Tom: Father, we don't have the authority over this spirit, but You do. Father, I thank You for the shed blood of Jesus Christ. (Sinister laughing.)

Theta: (Chanting.) Kill him dead . . . shoot him in the head. (Repeated many times.)

Tom: Go away. Bring David out. ("I hate you!") Bind him right now, in the name of Jesus Christ. Make him weak, I pray. Set him completely aside. Enable Rick to give up his foothold.

Rick: I don't want to go through the casket.

Tom: The casket is an awful thing, Rick, and we're not denying your right to feel bad about it. There's pain, there's anger, there's hurt. There's a foothold there, isn't there? Can you say, "I renounce the foothold Satan has on the casket."

Rick: I renounce the foothold Satan has on the casket. (Shuffling noises and sinister laughter.)

Theta: I fool you every time! (Repeats that.)

Tom: In the name of Jesus Christ, set this spirit aside. Rick, are you ready to renounce Theta and all his spirits? Can you say, "I love Jesus, and I renounce Theta and the three spirits under him"?

Rick: I love Jesus, and I renounce Theta and the three spirits under him.

Tom: Okay, now. (Intense groaning is heard.) Jason, Mr. Macquet, Philip, Byron, and everyone inside, all together . . . (Groaning.) let's together say, "Theta and the spirits under you, in the name of Jesus I command you to leave." (Groaning continues.) "In the name of Jesus I command you to leave."

Rick: In the name of Jesus I command you to leave.

Tom: Okay, Theta, your foothold is gone. In the name of Jesus you must go.

Theta: I don't have to. What if I just want to? (Jeers.) Then you don't have anything to say about it, do you?

Tom: Lord Jesus, send this spirit where he belongs, right now, we pray in the name and in the authority of Jesus Christ.

Theta: Maybe I don't want to be here any more.

Tom: Then go. In the name, power and authority of Jesus, Theta, begone. You, the three under you, and whoever else you have in Rick, we command you all to leave now, in the name of Jesus Christ. Anyone else who's there, we command you to leave.

Theta: If I go, it won't be because you tell me to.

Tom: Father, show this spirit his arrogance is unwarranted. "At the name of Jesus every knee will bow, every tongue will confess that Jesus Christ is Lord, to the glory of God the Father" (a Scripture passage.) The devil's time is short, and your time is over. Theta, begone, in the name of Jesus Christ, we command you. Leave right now. (Uhhhhh! Ahhhh!) Leave, right now, in the name of Jesus Christ. All the way out! Go. Go where Jesus sends you. (Groaning continues.) Rick, tell them to leave. Philip, Byron and Jason. Mr. Macquet, Shelby, all of you, tell them to go.

Rick: (Weakly.) Go, Theta. (Groaning.)

Tom: Go out, Theta! All the way. Leave Rick unharmed.

Rick: Go! In the name of Jesus, go!

Tom: I claim the protection of the shed blood of Jesus. (Intense, "Ahhh ... Oooooh.") Go all the way out. Theta, you and your horde, all at once! (Panting is heard.)

Rick: Oh, thank you, God! (Crying in happiness.)

Tom: Can I talk to Philip? How are you feeling, Philip? Did you see those spirits leave?

Philip: Yes.

Tom: You saw the power of God, didn't you?

Philip: Especially over the one that uses my name. He was ugly. He was all wet and greasy looking.

Tom: Rick, I want to be your friend. You're a special guy. You did pretty good in a hard situation. With Theta around, it's been tough, hasn't it? I want to commend you, Rick.

Rick: When he left, he was crying, and his three friends were laughing at him. He was afraid. He was slithering. He was in trouble. He was in trouble.

Tom: God has done a big miracle today, Rick. A big miracle.

11

RICK HAMMOND:
Spiritual
warfare

PART II. About Exorcism

Jim: One question came to my mind as Theta and his hordes were leaving: Was that *you* in pain, or was that only the sound of a departing spirit in pain?

Rick: That was more me in pain—physical and emotional—than it was the creatures. It was very painful. It felt like my skin were being ripped off, peeled off, from the inside. It felt as if there were an actual physical attachment. The sensation was like that gravelly type of sound you get when you pull velcro apart—like being skinned from the inside.

Jim: Wow! That must have been awful! How long did it take you to get a sense that you had recovered?

Rick: Forty-five minutes to an hour. As soon as the creatures were gone, the physical pain stopped.

Jim: How did that session change your life, or how has it been different since then?

Rick: That was the second to last exorcism.* By that time, and shortly after that, most of the creature activity was over. I guess

---

*   See my first book for more on sequestered spirits. Demons tend to be cast out in clusters, but other spirits can remain hidden. Their points of attachment seem to be dissociated memories or vows and they are not the two strongest emotions I had following that were the deep sense of shame that I had been used in that way, and the first real grief for myself. I had been limited in my life, and I felt a sense of loss as I realized that a great deal of my life had been handicapped by those kind of experiences.

Jim: How long ago was that exorcism?

Rick: A year and a half ago.

Jim: What would you say to people who ask you whether Theta and his hordes tried to return and harass you?

Rick: Like any other Christian, I am in a constant battle. I have a clear sense of what that battle is, and the reality of it hasn't left me. But now the battle takes place on the outside of me, as opposed to it being inside.

For the first time, as a Christian, I was able to *do* something about the attack. There had been such a feeling of powerlessness, of total vulnerability—they could do whatever they wanted to do. There was no sense of having victory against Satan, as a Christian, until that time.

Jim: I am pretty certain that non-Christian psychologists will say, "That lack of control—that powerlessness—was simply your alters fighting with each other."

Rick: My experience was not that my alters would fight with one another, they seemed to defer to one another. I had a very strong sense of my alters being supportive and not being enemies. They were friends, in every sense of the word. Whatever struggle there was among them, or whatever level of competition existed, it was designed *by* them for my welfare.

Jim: They weren't fighting with each other at all?

Rick: I can't say that. There was competition; there was a sense of, "Let me do that for you. You aren't creative enough, or designed to do that." From an outsider's viewpoint it may appear that they were fighting with one another, but it was more a sense of, "Who's going to take the hit?"

---

removable until those memories are uncovered.

Jim: How would you contrast that with the demonic harassment that was going on that you had no control over?

Rick: They were trying to kill me! They were trying to destroy me. It always involved severe mental and physical pain. Through the years of therapy the attacks became more violent. By the time the MPD and the demonic element were discovered, they had become physically aggressive with me, and had devised a cycle of plans for self-destruction. From the time I realized what was going on with me, I knew the difference between alters who were struggling to gain control so my system would be safe, and the demonic element.

After they were disclosed, after I became willing to say, as a Christian it is possible for a person to be demonized, the struggle became overt, intense and physical, and I was able immediately to distinguish whether it was demons who were trying to destroy. I had no alters who were set on my destruction. [In conversation later, Tom told me that alters can sometimes be destructive, but *behind* the urges are usually demonic pressures.]

Jim: That may be a real guiding point for a lot of readers.

Rick: It is, because, Jim, I am actually convinced that dissociation is a gift. It's not a curse. It's a gift. It has to be given back, in a sense, because it's accomplished its work. I think the very essence of dissociation is self-preservation.

Jim: So when it is destructive, you assume it is coming from the outside, from the demonic?

Rick: Dissociation does involve many opportunities for demonic involvement, because as a split-up person, you don't have the spiritual wherewithall to recognize it, or to deal with it. The nature of dissociation as I experienced it was that when the fight becomes tough, you quit! Instead of continuing the struggle, you'd rather quit. So an alter would first deny the whole issue, then an alter like Mr. Macquet would try to reason very logically, then Byron would try to block it.

Jim: No wonder you were so vulnerable. There was not enough strength in any one of them to withstand the demonic.

Rick: None at all.

THE PASTORAL COUNSELOR

Jim: Who was that pastoral counselor?

Rick: Someone who came on the scene right at the beginning of this process. He was one of a group of men who came to our house for a prayer meeting. We had contacted Dr. Dickason in Chicago—he was the only person I knew of who had knowledge about any of this. So he had given us the names of a couple of people here, in whom he had confidence. We had contacted them, and a group came to our home to intercede in my behalf. Tom Hawkins was a member of that group. I hadn't known him before that time.

Jim: This man then became your therapist?

Rick: He is a pastor.

Jim: And he helped you all the way through?

Rick: That's right.

Jim: He was sent to you, practically by God, wasn't he?

Rick: No question about that. There were a couple of prayer meetings for me, and he was in the second one. The other people were trying to cast out alters. My behavior suggested to these men that they were dealing with demons. As it turned out they were dealing with frightened, intimidated, antagonistic alters, trying to cast them out. And the more they tried to do that, the more aggressive the alters became.

Jim: I can understand that.

Rick: That meeting lasted about ten hours. Tom, in the midst of all of this, kept coming to me. I was in my bedroom. They were all in our bedroom. He kept coming to me right at the edge of the bed, very quietly saying, "I know you are not demonic. I know you need to be validated." He was very calming, very soothing, and very comforting. And he gained a great deal of my trust in the first few hours.

They all left that night, and the next morning my wife and I were sitting in our living room talking, praying, and discussing our options, and I said to her, "Of all the people we have had contact with to this point, if that man (I didn't even know his name), if that tall man would come to our door, if God would send him to our house this morning, I believe he is someone I could talk with." Jim, within a matter of seconds our doorbell rang, and Tom was there!

Jim: Amazing.

Rick: And from that point on, he and I began meeting two or three times a week for two or three or four hours sometimes.

He had been involved in the therapy of a number of multiples—they had been seeing him for teatment. Tom has since left the pastorate to specialize in MPD and to help pastors and churches better support people who are working through dissociative disorders and ritual abuse. So he came to me with a great deal of experience in this area.

Jim: Let me step back here. What was it like for you to have parts of you identified as demonic? Did you believe those people who said you might have some demonic stuff in you?

Rick: I had no other option. I knew nothing about MPD. Nothing. All I knew about MPD was what has been shot across the television screen.

Jim: Which isn't very accurate.

Rick: Which isn't very accurate. My reaction to it always was, if this is a reality, it's certainly rare. And of course at that time I had no reason to believe that I fell into the category of persons who would dissociate. I had no information, no recollection of any trauma in my life at all.

Jim: That's the way dissociation works, isn't it?

Rick: But I had no reason to even *suspect* it. So I had only two options. One was insanity, and I knew I wasn't crazy. The tests proved that. The other was I could be demonic—Dickason had given me enough theological material to believe that it was a possibility for me. So I came to those experiences believing *that* was the problem.

Jim: And this man of mercy came to you then, right after you said to your wife that you could trust him, so you began to work with him. Did he explain to you what MPD is like, so you could understand it?

Rick: He began sharing, very generally describing my situation without giving it a name, and the more he talked, the more I identified with what he was describing. And so finally I said to him, "What you are describing is what I experience on a daily basis, and what I have experienced all my life." It was only then that he began using the MPD vocabulary.

Jim: The tape indicated that not only did he have a good grasp of MPD, but he also knew about the influence of evil spirits. And did he let you know, in the beginning, that he was familiar with both the psychological and the spiritual domains?

Rick: Yes.

Jim: Was that comforting to you or was it scary?

Rick: It was scary to me because I had alters who were very much into protecting me from any of that sort of reality. I had alters who were extremely competitive, some of whom wanted me to believe I was crazy. I had demonized alters who had convinced me that the ultimate fruition was to take your own life, and had managed to persuade me against any other possibility. I had alters who were absolutely committed to secrecy. There were a few who were responsive, but the majority, at least early on, were not, and they wanted to believe that this was pretend! So I wasn't real cooperative.

Jim: It sounds like it's an understatement to say that you had a hard time sticking with the therapy. How did you . . . *why* did you stay in?

Rick: I guess I became absolutely convinced. God kept putting substantial evidence in front of my eyes that I could not ignore. And by that time the memories were starting to come. I always referred to it as "falling out."

Jim: Falling out! That's a good description. Memories seem sometimes to just drop down from . . . who knows where?

Rick: Those memories were coming, and they were so devastating to me that it was imperative to find some solution. I knew from my own psychological background that, if those memories were true, if they were accurate, they would have a devastating effect upon me. Also, some of the alters were won to Christ and became cooperative. David did not really want to be in therapy because it was so extremely painful. I always referred to those initial recollections not as memories, but as events, because they were events to me. It was as if, when an event occurred in my childhood, an alter was created to respond to that event, and a shell was put around the event. When those shells began to break down, I had the physical, the mental, the spiritual and the emotional reactions I'd had when the event occurred. So they weren't memories to me. They were events. After the event was experienced, it became a memory—an unpleasant one, but still just a memory. There was a great deal going on inside of me—critical alters who used theological jargon, quoting the apostle Paul's passages about forgetting the past, and the use-lessness of delving into all this madness—this "nonsense."

Jim: Your alters were using the Scriptures against you?

Rick: Absolutely. Not all the alters wanted to be in therapy, so they did that to prevent me from staying in.

Jim: That really is self-defeating!

Rick: That was probably the greatest barrier to my therapy— what I thought I knew. I have a psychological background, as well as this theological background, so I had some alters who used every bit of information they could muster to torpedo the whole process. They quoted Scriptures in Greek and in Hebrew in order to block me.

Jim: Was it therapy itself, the uncovering of the events, that kept you coming back to get more healing?

Rick: Yes. Because when the event was processed, I experienced immediate relief. It was as if a pressure point—and there were hundreds of them—it was as if a pressure point was relieved. The response was that on occasion I could actually breathe better. All kinds of physical relief would come. I suffered all my life from horrendous headaches. I have been in the hospital probably twenty-five or thirty times but I never was diagnosed with any identifiable problem at all. I have been rushed to the hospital again and again in ambulances, or my family has had to rush me there, but as those hidden events came out and were processed, the physical symptoms began to disappear. So that's what kept me coming back, even though it was extremely painful. I never knew what I was going to experience in a particular session, yet knowing I had survived it *once* helped me realize I would survive it a second time. I knew I wouldn't have to go through it a third time, because it would indeed be over. That kept bringing me back.

Jim: Well, thank God it was so successful for you. You know, a lot of people are already familiar with multiple personality, but they think there is no such thing as a demon. They say those are simply malevolent personalities—you know, nasty folks inside of you who eventually are going to have to be brought together inside of you, and united with the rest of you. So these non-believing-in-demons people think that, if you cast demons out, they will only come back at some later time as a personality, because they weren't demons in the first place. What would you say to those people?

Rick: Well, my own experience is that none did. There were probably 250 demonic spirits in me that were exorcised, and none of them has come back. And with each exorcism, I moved to a higher level of ability to function, even with the negative alters I had, and I had several.

Jim: So there *were* so-called malevolent personalities in you?

Rick: Oh, yes.

Jim: And you saw that they were different from the evil spirits?

Rick: Oh, yes! They responded to the gospel—they responded to spiritual information. My theological understanding of this process, Jim, is that what we are talking about when we talk about a malevolent alter is, we are talking about a part of Rick that had not been brought to captivity in Christ. So their conversion, and sometimes I put this in quotes, their "conversion," I view as part of my own personal sanctification. The parts of me that had not actively, consciously participated in Rick's conversion now began to experientially take part in my regeneration.

Jim: I think Jesus' teaching may overlap your experience here. In Luke chapter 11 He taught about letting the light of God come into every area of your life. Is that what you are describing here?

Rick: Exactly. The demonic powers were not responsive to that. In fact they tried—and on occasion would pretend—to be responsive to God's power. But when they were tested, they could not deny who they were. There was a clear distinction. A great deal of imagery helped me distinguish alters from demons. A certain amount of spiritual discernment—that may be gifted-ness—enabled me to do that.

I have experienced the same thing when involved with other people. While I was in graduate school classes, we were in settings where therapists were dealing with other multiples, and I consistently could distinguish between demons and alters as the therapist worked with the people. I have also been able to do that since integration.

Jim: So you didn't lose this spiritual awareness after you finished integration?

Rick: I haven't.

Jim: I know that has been suggested by Dr. Colin Ross in his book on treatment for MPD. He wrote that something about the dividedness overlaps spiritual awareness, or telepathy, or other paranormal things. And he hypothesizes that paranormal experiences should probably disappear when therapy concludes, when unification has taken place. But you have found that to be just the opposite?

Rick: It has been for me.

Jim: So you have had more and more spiritual awareness and discernment, and the ability to recognize the ways other people are being spiritually attacked?

Rick: Yes. I don't know if that will be everyone's experience. All I can say is, it's mine. Early on, before integration, we were in sessions with two or three multiples. We were observing or participating on their behalf. Sometimes when the therapist was dealing with the multiple, I would have a sense, a feeling within myself, a desire to tell the therapist, "You are not talking to an alter here. This is a spirit." But I would resist that because it sounded foolish to me. It sounded like all the things I am afraid of. It would sound weird, yet it would become such a strong sense in me I would begin to feel I was doing a disservice by not saying anything. So I would pose it very gently. "Could you possibly be talking to a demon instead of an alter? Would you consider that as a possibility, and perhaps change your approach?" And as they did—and we are talking about five or six or eight occasions here—as they did that, they would discover that a change in approach was needed. The interesting thing about it, Jim, is that before integration, when I would do that, and an evil spirit would be discovered, *I* would be attacked, physically. I would experience physical symptoms while the therapist was dealing with the demonic element in the other multiple. I would suffer terribly. Since integration, that sense of discernment is still there, but there is no longer a physical attack.

Jim: That is really interesting!

Rick: I don't know what any of that means. I haven't had a chance to put a theological perspective to that. I haven't talked to anyone except you and my wife! I don't know what to do with that, but them there's the facts.

Jim: It sounds to me like another point in Scripture, where Jesus said He has come to set the captives free, is illustrated—you were still in chains while a demonized multiple, but you are free now.

Rick: The logic seems to me, you cannot step into that realm as a multiple, or as a demonized multiple, without coming back with a heightened sense of what this is all about.

Jim: Certainly. Now, how have the benefits of your growth and improvement spread, maybe to your family or friends?

Rick: Well, I am a nice guy right now!

Jim: That's no joke! You sound like a nice guy. But how has this influenced other people? Do you see God promoting health in other people through your experience?

Rick: All of my alters were distinctly separated—none of them overlapped, and they were all very distinct. I didn't have any kind of middle-of-the-road alters who were normal. They each had an unusual if not unique way, their own strategy about them. And in talking with people now, when I offer to them specific examples of how they may have seen Byron, or how they may have seen Jason, their eyes light up and they say, "Oh, yeah!

I remember that!" So there is a real sense of recognition by people as I give them specific information about the formerly separate alters.

I think of Eric, our son who is 15. He just wrote three or four pages for me. I asked him to sit down while it was still fresh, and write some of his ideas and recollections and feelings about living with me through the years, and especially the last year and a half. His perspective is quite positive. He knew that part of me was a Christian, but he was pretty sure that part of me wasn't. He wrote he had seen blending, or the smoothing out of those rough spots in me. Our daughter Michelle has been away at college during this period of time, so she hasn't had the experience of living with an integrated father, so it will be interesting over Christmas break and spring break to see what her reactions are.

For the most part, the people we share with are positive, but I think it puts them in an awkward position because they are not sure how to respond. That's presenting some challenges.

Jim: You mean before, even though you were somewhat moody, they considered that you were at least an okay guy. But now that you are a recovered multiple, they look on you with suspicion, or are more hesitant to trust you than they were before?

Rick: I don't think it's trust as much as it is that they don't know my level of fragility. They stay at a distance. At least that's my perspective.

Jim: Have you played that tape of the exorcism for people? If so, can they believe it? Can they profit from it?

Rick: We played it probably for fifty people at various times, in groups. Down the line, the reaction has been positive. I have been very pointed in saying to them, whether you believe this or not, is no test of our friendship, but I do want to know what you think, and most have responded, "Yes. We believe this."

Jim: It's pretty compelling, isn't it?

Rick: Yes, it is. Peoples' response has been interesting. It's believable. I think a lot of that, though, has to do with their knowledge of me. I am the last person in the world who would believe this. I am a conservative guy, cut and dried—a "give me theology before anything else" kind of guy, and keep your emotion on the sidelines, if you have to have *any at all!* Just give me the facts, and nothing but the facts.

Jim: You weren't cut out for this role in any way?

Rick: Right. Give me Greek and theology, and leave me alone. I have never displayed emotion. In a counseling situation I can be warm and personable. I am not suggesting that I'm a cold duck, but in terms of expressing my own faith, it's pretty cut and dried.

Jim: Does listening to the tape help the people who hear it? I mean, do they get closer to God because of your sharing with them, or do they sort of keep it all in their head, and say, "Well, maybe I saw something like that on '60 Minutes' "?

Rick: No. It remains to be seen if they get closer to God. All I can do is share some of their comments. Thinking in terms of two or three groups we have played it for, I have heard comments like, "Rick, how can we tell if our children are being hurt like you were hurt as a child? What do we need to know? What are the signs? How can we tell if we need to be more careful with the people we allow our children to be with?" They also ask questions about what the church can do. They show that sort of concern.

One of the other things they often ask is, "What can we do for you?" We haven't met with a group who have not had two or three people say, "Okay, Rick, we appreciate your letting us in on what has happened to you. What do you need now? What can we do for you now? Where are you now?" The response to the disclosure has been very positive. We have not, to date, had one negative response. On a scale of 1 to 10, I'd say it's been 8 and above.

Jim: Now, another question: What can churches do?

Rick: I think essentially, teach. It goes further than a theology of Satan and angels. We need teaching that begins with what I will call the normal ramifications of spiritual warfare. Not everybody is MPD; not everybody is demonized; but every Christian lives in a hostile environment because of the fall of man and the presence of the devil and his angels.

Jim: That hits close to home for me, Rick. I grew up as a preacher's kid, and when missionaries would come from the third world countries and talk about demons, I would say, "Oh, yeah. That's interesting." But I would never think about demons wanting to come to America! It would never be anything I would expect to see.

Rick: We should be teaching along the lines of the ramifications of the warfare we are all involved in. I think we hit too softly in this area. Some issues we hit hard, and rightly so. When it comes to abortion and pornography, we hit hard and tough, and we need to do that. But when it comes to this whole area of what it means to be a believer living in a world where Satan rules, even though temporarily, most of us don't know what it means on a practical level. So when it happens to us, we don't even identify it as that. We use an entirely different vocabulary to describe demonic oppression, one that is mixed in with a good psychological vocabulary, but I think we need to develop a lexicon for describing what it is like to be oppressed by the devil.

Jim: So how can the church help people learn to identify the devil's activity in their lives?

Rick: I think it goes back to the leadership, and their willingness to take the risk of going a little deeper than what seems safe to talk about. As Christians, we are capable of being terribly unkind to one another through the labeling process. Anything you can't wrap a Bible verse around is suspect. And we haven't been willing to say if we even believe in the supernatural aspect. We don't want to step out and risk the kind of labeling that brings. But there are some experiences that verses just won't wrap around.

Jim: So we have to go one step further than just trying to find the right verse?

Rick: Right. We have got to be willing to listen to what people are telling us and respond to it without labeling them. I'm a reasonably intelligent person, and pretty capable, but I am terribly intimidated by what people think about me. There were times in my life when I was absolutely suicidal, and I needed to *say* that to somebody. I needed to tell somebody, but I frequently would be willing to just go ahead and kill myself rather than risk being labeled as depressed, or crazy, or unspiritual.

Jim: People were labeling you to the point where you could not even share openly about your struggles?

Rick: I didn't tell them. I suffered in isolation. I was afraid to tell the people I should have been able to tell most freely. I was afraid to say, "This is what's going on in my life, and I need some help."

Jim: What will it take for people to profit from what you are saying?

Rick: I think it takes people who have some credibility to have the courage to stand up and say these things. I'm not sure I am there yet, but I sure want to be. On the negative side, it may take somebody who stands up with a gun in his hand in a communion service, like I was frequently tempted to do, and just shooting his head off, and leaving a note behind that says, "I came to you for help, and you didn't help." That was in my mind for probably the last ten or twelve years.

Jim: You were thinking of ending your life in the middle of a church service?

Rick: The idea was planted in my mind that the most destructive thing I could do would be to stand up in the middle of a communion service and shoot my head off. In fact, about six months before integration, I bought a gun to do just that. Imagine the impact that would have!

Jim: That would blow the church apart.

Rick: Yes.

Jim: And those people maybe would not have an ounce of faith left in them.

Rick: To leave a note behind explaining that "this is my response to what you guys have done for me" is obviously satanic. I'm not offering that as a way to alert the church, mind you, but I think of the desperation felt by so many people. One thing that really strikes me is that I had probably as many resources as anybody could possibly have. I think of the hundreds—thousands of people who are on the perimeter of the church looking in, who could be dubbed crazy, weird, strange, all those mean words we assign to people because they cannot control their behaviors or their moods. And we prefer that these people—if they come to church at all—stand at the outside edge. I was in the inner circle, but I felt very much an outsider.

Jim: So here you were a pastor, you had a supportive family and a good relationship with your wife, and a lot of people in the church supported you, and you *still* felt that way?

Rick: Absolutely. I knew just how they would respond if I told them that at times I was suicidal. I would lose my job. That was the first thing I always thought. If I go to an elder in my church, or any church, or if I go to the dean of students at a seminary or Bible school I was attending, and say to that person, "I don't know what's going on with me, but I frequently have this urge to throw myself in front of a car," the initial reaction would have been to take my job away from me, or to throw me out of school.

You can't do that, so you develop other ways of coping, and it builds up inside you, and builds up inside you, and builds up inside you, until you begin to think only in terms of how you can express that rage. For me, I never expressed my rage outwardly. I expressed it inwardly and always became self-destructive.

So I knew all the people, Jim. I knew the rules. I knew the original biblical languages. I knew the theology. I had all kinds of networking, and I was in a place where I could have—I should have—been able to get help immediately without taking any risks at all.

But I didn't feel free to do that. Then what about other people—dozens of other people with MPD that we know of, what do those people, who don't have those kinds of resources, do?

Jim: My goodness! I wonder how many people you have met in the last couple of years who also fall into the MPD category, who also may be demonized.

Rick: Lots of them. Lots of them.

Jim: Average folks? Folks from your church? Where do you meet these people?

Rick: I have been involved in the counseling ministry for the last three years in this area. There are lots of them.

Jim: So how does a church respond to that now? Are they enlightened? Are they ready to say, "Okay, we understand this now and we are ready to pitch in"?

Rick: That's a long way off, I think. Many people in my church are learning the language. I have some credibility. Some people believe me. They have known me. I have a good record, and have been a capable, functioning, producing kind of person. But we know people whose situations have rendered them so dysfunctional that they don't even have the ability to articulate their need, or they can't articulate it in any acceptable way. Their theology may be a little shaky; they may use bad language; they may not have the reverence for certain things that others hold reverent—and those behaviors get them dead ears.

Jim: You know, this is a real tragedy, Rick.

Rick: Yes, it is.

Jim: You have people obsessed with killing themselves, unable to articulate their pain very well, and here are God's chosen people who are not even intersecting with that. They aren't noticing it. They are not recognizing it. What's it going to take? How can God's people learn how to help these struggling, fractured folks?

Rick: It's interesting—just shortly before my integration, there was strong temptation on my part to make a deal internally. If all of the alters in me would cooperate with integration, and if all of the spirits would be willing to go away and leave me alone and never come back so I would be allowed to get well, I would keep my mouth shut. I wouldn't say word one. I just would go on with my life and be a well, whole, healthy person. That urge in me became extremely strong because I wanted so much to get well. But it's questionable whether they all would have kept their part of the agreement.

Jim: So you would have gone into isolation, then, about this topic? You would have just gone on and lived your life as though multiplicity and demonization had never happened to you?

Rick: I would have taken my healing, and gone into silence.

Jim: So why didn't you do that?

Rick: I was always sure of one thing throughout all this period of time since my conversion: I knew I was a child of God. That was never an issue with me. The second thing I was sure of was my call to ministry. Those two certainties in my life are the things that kept me from making that deal.

Jim: So you are still in the ministry?

Rick: Yes. I am finishing my master's degree in theology.

Jim: Are you able to get people motivated to come alongside and work with you to help suffering people?

Rick: That remains to be seen. It's still a little early for me to know. I'm just sort of "coming out," if you know what I mean.

Jim: You told me a few days ago that so many Christians are interested in all this, but knowing about it doesn't seem to affect them. Could you explain that?

Rick: In my thinking there's a difference between Christians who are curious about things they have heard about all their lives, and those who want to have contact with them and test their own sense of reality. Maybe that's an initial step in getting involved, I'm not sure. I don't think curiosity is a bad thing. I think the people we are in contact with now, and are sharing with, could be described as having a healthy curiosity. Not a morbid curiosity—we haven't had people asking personal, detailed, morbid-type questions about the abuse. The questions have been more along the lines of, What does it feel like to dissociate? What does it feel like to be integrated? How has that changed your life? Those kinds of questions. That probably is a necessary step. Now we need to go on to step two. Now that we understand a little about this, we need to try to get placement for people who need a place to live because it's not safe for them to be at home. Or maybe get jobs for those people who have lost their jobs because they can't function consistently. That's the level I would like to see the church come to.

I believe there are lay people in the local church who have a certain variety of spiritual gifts, who could be trained to do this work. I really believe that. I'm certainly not suggesting that people who have your level of training are not fit enough to do this work, but you professional guys—there just are not enough of you to do this.

Jim: Yes, that's been a real problem. Especially lately, I have felt overwhelmed.

Rick: I'll bet.

Jim: There aren't enough therapists to go around. Literally hundreds of people are looking for the right therapist, and maybe they will have to turn to a program such as you describe, with the lay people doing the core of the work.

Rick: I envision a time when a highly trained, psychologically oriented therapist, in addition to his own private practice, would be willing to take on the responsibility of training a selected group of gifted lay people, supervising their work, and being available for consultations. We should not turn this work over to untrained lay people, to just sort of mish-mash and fly through it. But if the whole area of MPD, particularly the demonic involvement, has such significant spiritual ramifications, my belief system tells me that God has equipped the church to deal with it. From a practical standpoint, I envision a time when Christian therapists, as part of their ministry, will train gifted lay people in local churches to at least do the support work and the on-going crisis management that's involved.

Jim: The survivors need a lot of help, don't they?

Rick: Much more then they can get in a therapist's office in an hour and a half.

Jim: One of my colleagues said he thinks it takes about fifty people in the church *per MPD client*, to be able to cover all the clients' needs—taking care of the car and the lawn mower, and what happens when a window breaks? They have nobody in their systems to do those things, and they need to be able to call folks in the church and say, "Hey, can you help me get my car door open?" Anything like that. How to manage a budget. How to *make up* a budget, for that matter.

Rick: If that kind of support were available, I believe the therapeutic process would become much more efficient, and not as time consuming as it is now. I came to one point where I literally had to make a decision to shut my entire system of personalities down because of my other responsibilities. And when I shut the system down, it was tough to get it activated again. When I shut it down, I did it in such a manageable and organized way that I was convinced there was no reason to reactivate it. If I could shut it down and control it that capably, then I could go on and live as a multiple the rest of my life. So it was necessary for me to make a positive decision to keep my system open, as difficult, as painful, and as crazy as it made our lives.

We literally, daily, here in our home, went from one crisis to another. There were times when I did nothing but switch. And my children, Michelle and Eric, and my wife, Stathia, became my loving therapists as they identified alters, validated them, talked with them, urged them, loved them, dealt with them, confronted them and exhorted them! I have dozens and dozens and dozens of memories of sitting at our dinner table with my son and daughter calling me Byron, and telling me what I needed to hear.

Jim: How beautiful.

Rick: And of Byron talking to Eric as his equal, learning from him and getting advice from him. Byron was going to be around the rest of my life, so he had to learn how to live in this house. And as Byron became more and more comfortable, knowing he was liked even though he was aggressive and had some negative aspects to his character, he was accepted. Eric and Michelle came to love Byron as much as they love Rick, the dad.

Jim: That really advances progress in therapy.

Rick: There was no reason for Byron to insist on a separate place in my life, or our home. Primarily, my family's ministry to me made him realize that, if he wanted to be around and out, his best chance for doing that was to be willing to rejoin me.

Jim: Perfect! What do you have to say, Rick, to the person who is a multiple, who is having a difficult time in therapy, and is thinking of shutting down the system, to remain a multiple for the rest of his or her life, ununited?

Rick: I have two things to say. The first thing would be, I have a lot of empathy for people who are thinking that, and I would want to let them know that. I could understand that kind of thinking. And I *know* that would seem to be very logical in some instances.

The second thing I would say is that I believe God created us to be a whole person. Not separate. Not part and parcel. A whole person. And if I want to live an abundant life, my greatest potential for doing that is as a whole, integrated person. When God made me, he designed me to be one person with one personality.

We live in a fallen world, and as a result, I, and a lot of other people, have been subjected to horrendous experiences as children. God's gift to us in those experiences was the ability to dissociate. I firmly believe the dissociation is a gift. It is not a curse. It is a gift. But, as I become wiser and stronger and more mature, if I am not led back to the process so that those events can be experienced as a mature adult, then instead of being a gift to me, dissociation can become a curse. We become vulnerable to satanic and demonic involvement because we don't have all of our resources to defend us.

So here is a traumatized child who dissociates and creates an alter who, in order to handle the trauma, is extremely aggressive. Very unlikeable. Very obnoxious. That part of me will not be able to experience the fullness of life Christ intended me to have until he is willing to share totally in my experience.

Not integrating, and shutting the system down effectively, would be second best. I can understand the thinking of a person who is tired of being misunderstood and of the frustration of being misdiagnosed for years. And I know how that kind of thinking, the idea of a shutdown, can be appealing and logical. But my theology steps in, and then my experience steps in to say, if God's intent and design is for me to live an abundant life as a unified, whole person, then it can be done.

12

ELIZABETH POWER*:
Each Day
Is for Living

ELIZABETH WAS my ally before I even knew her name. During the question and answer time at a seminar where I was a featured presenter, she helped me with some questions that were too tough for me—and she was in the audience! She had an amazing amount of information immediately available on any aspect of MPD, no matter how remote or obscure. She was fully informed about the spiritual side of the MPD picture, too, and she talked about her walk with God in terms nobody could miss. She loves God. I very much appreciated her input at the seminar, as each of her contributions enriched the discussion and was presented in an unmistakably helpful style.

Somewhere at the conference it was mentioned that she too is a multiple. That did not catch me off guard. I had already met enough multiples to know of the things they can accomplish, and she had clearly demonstrated her mastery of the material before she was identified as a multiple.

That was last fall, before the central concept of this book had come into focus for me. At that time I was planning to include only unified multiples as participants in the book. I had been challenged to demonstrate that the therapy described in my first book is truly successful, by finding people who have used it and

---

* Elizabeth Power can be contacted at the MPD/DD Resource and
   Information Center, by calling (615) 327-1510.

who have reached "stable integration." I was willing to take the challenge, but I soon found that (1) it limited me by excluding people like Elizabeth, and (2) it contradicted the central concept in this way: If a multiple is truly splendid, that should be apparent before he (or she) reaches unity; the splendidness might be overlooked altogether if we considered any positive qualities only *after* treatment is finished. It would, frankly, be a more powerful statement to interview people who are splendid despite their dividedness. Such was the case with Elizabeth, and she opened up a few hours to develop a chapter with me, even though she is the CEO of two businesses and often gives her leftover time to hurting people.

* * *

Jim: What is life like for you these days?

Elizabeth: It's interesting. Sometimes it's too full. Today, for example, I've just come home after working with a psychotherapist. I am helping her reorganize and streamline her practice, using the things I use on the inside—systems management, identifying and managing processes, looking at how things are organized and how things work. I had a lot of help from a lot of different selves in working with her today.

She has two offices, and five clinicians work for her. I was putting her billing system on her computer, going through all the thinking necessary to set up her accounting. In a group practice you only see the surface of the accounting, but, like a multiple, there are layers and layers and layers of detail, behind the surface information. The users of the program only see the surface. They don't need to see the layers you have to think through. Helping them learn to think and to see the levels of detail, and the four-dimensional matrices they have to think in, is what we've been doing at her practice today.

Jim: Oh, boy! And this is a Saturday! You said you had finished a manuscript for publication only yesterday?

Elizabeth: Yes, I've been working on a book for a month. It's called *Managing Our Selves: Building a Community of Caring*. It is a self-management workbook for multiples that doesn't mess at all with people's traumas. Instead, it helps them look purely at how to manage their systems. We set it up to be very usable, and when I say "we," I mean *I*, editors on the outside who've helped me, and the folks on the inside who've helped write it. The text on the left-hand pages focuses on a particular topic, like "Letting Your Self Learn"; "Thinking About MPD"; "Self-Image and Selves"; "Travel Issues"; "Sitting Ducks and Swamps"; and, "Managing Triggers." The right hand side of those pages has a couple of process questions, written so that any self who happens to be reading has a chance at answering.

Jim: That's very practical.

Elizabeth: Exceptionally practical. Just helping people to learn how to get through the day is critical! Back on the first of January I opened up, in addition to E. Power and Associates, which is a consulting and training firm that works mostly in industry, the Multiple Personality Disorder/Dissociative Disorders [MPD/DD] Resource and Education Center. The mission of this center is to provide consultation, education, and prevention services to clients, clinicians and the community for the purpose of reducing the time, cost and trauma required to heal from MPD and dissociative disorders.

Jim: That is right down our alley! I will certainly make that reference and address available, if you send it to me. [See footnote on page 165.]

Elizabeth: You've got it! We already have made a presentation about MPD and spirituality at a psychotherapy institute workshop, which is a secular organization. We were working with clinicians, from a wide variety of spiritual preferences, on how to relate dissociation and spirituality. Our goal was to help them realize that not all dissociative experiences are pathological, and that religious experiences are often dissociative.

Jim: That's a pretty big hunk you bit off and chewed!

Elizabeth: Why not!? I've got a lot of help. What can I say?

Jim: Tell us about your help.

Elizabeth: As you know, Jim, I'm a "Poly-Fragmented Complex Multiple With Post-Traumatic Stress Disorder." That's a mouthful, and what it really means is that I come with a crowd. Everyone on the inside is learning to use similar speech patterns and mannerisms, so that other folks will be more comfortable. When it's appropriate, like doing an all-day seminar, or working on a complex project, a variety of selves may help in different ways, including contributing more varied facial expressions.

People ask, "Well, are you going to integrate?"

My views are: "Integration" and "fusion" are static terms. Personally, I prefer to focus on conformity to Christ in a healthy way as an outcome, rather than on fusion and integration.

Jim: So if "fusion" and "integration" are static, do you use some terms that are more dynamic?

Elizabeth: In thinking through this process, I'm most comfortable with the fact that I am one human being with multiple centers of perception. I'd much rather think about "coalescing" and "clustering" than "fusion" and "integration." After all, since "integration" is something society has not been able to achieve during my lifetime, why should I? And "fusion" is a concept related to the bomb I've heard adults talking about since I was a little kid. "Clustering" and "coalescing" are not socially loaded—much more content neutral. Those are social concepts. If, however, I pursue conformity to Christ as my personal goal in healing, that frees me to express myself more broadly. This model is reflected in Jesus as part of the trinity—the Father, Son and Holy Spirit—which is three-in-one-inseparable, each different manifestations of the Godhead. If I continue pursuing conformity to Christ, I may end up—who knows?—three-in-one, five-in-one, eight-in-one, ten-in-one, each different manifestations of self, equally healthy.

Jim: How many manifestations do you currently have?

Elizabeth: About 160, and the reason I say "about" is, some are becoming known, and some are being joined together like in a marriage. When two become one, they are still equally two. They share each other's history, each other's knowledge, and they have a unified relationship in spirit. For instance, I once had Sarah and Sally, and now it's Sarah-Sally. When you call for one or the other, you get the "clump."

Jim: Did that togetherness happen automatically for them, or was it more of a decision?

Elizabeth: It took time to bring it about. What I find happening, Jim, is that I look at the process of management—building bridges and taking down barriers, beginning to help selves see how much they have in common. I look at the strength of the community within, the potential aspects, the strengths that are there. You have to have those to survive all those years, and I am grateful for all of them, every single alter. They all helped me get to where I am now. They all have inherent strengths and potentials, in addition to cognitive errors and "stuckness." When I focus on the strengths and the assets, they find they don't need to be so separate. They no longer need to vie for attention, or time and space, because they work together in a collaborative community. They all support each other, and the common good of the group. It seems they say, "We are doing the same thing, so why don't we cluster together? We can coalesce or blend our energies, and still have our separate histories. We can share simultaneously, take up less room, use less time, and still get our needs met." It becomes a natural coalescence.

Jim: How can they work together so well?

Elizabeth: What reason would they have to fight all the time? If they manage agreement instead of conflict, it's a whole lot easier. I get them together and ask them to look at the choices to be made: "Let's figure out what we're going to eat. Does anybody in there feel left out of the food-choosing process lately?" Maybe an internal hand goes up, and maybe not. I always remind every one of us, including the party with whom you're speaking, that there are a thousand and ninety-five meals a year, at three a day. Surely everybody can have something suitable to their taste sometime!

Jim: It sounds like there is an automatic willingness to give each other what they need.

Elizabeth: There is. It helped us when I began to point out how much choice we have. We look at the consequences, and at how much further we can get if we play "win-win" in our relationships. We are all customers and suppliers to each other. If I'm your supplier, and you're my customer, what do you need from me? Right now I'm supplying *you* with information. You're also *my* supplier, though, meeting some of my needs, being a customer of mine. What do I need from you to satisfy my needs? It's about reciprocity.

Jim: That sounds like a major step forward from what I have seen.

Elizabeth: Yes. It comes from my work as an organization development and management consultant in the business world. The biggest difference is, I'm dealing with an internal rather than an external organization.

Jim: But the way you organize it starts with cooperation.

Elizabeth: We all have common needs. The selves need to find common agreement about their issues. We need to have the healthiest fun, to meet the most needs everyone has within the common value system we've all agreed to, with the least guilt and shame possible.

Jim: You mentioned some things about spirituality. What has God been teaching you?

Elizabeth: I've seen God preparing me, during my whole life, to understand non-traditional experiences. When I read in Ephesians about reconciliation between Jew and Gentile, it makes perfect sense to me. I have to do that internally. He is the one who gives me Psalms for comfort, and He helps me understand that my shame will be turned to praise.

He gives me the story of Paul to help me understand how special I am to Him. What Paul went through as he confronted the horrors he had to deal with, having slaughtered Christians on a daily basis, is no different from the horror multiples go through—that I go through as I uncover different pieces of my history. I have to face the world outside every day, and the world inside, knowing who I am and what I've done. We're pursuing absolution and forgiveness, without sabotage. God, through His mercy, helps me understand that all things work together for good to them that love Him. He has shown that shame began in the Garden of Eden, and from that time forward, men and women have been taught lies, and have been believing lies about themselves. He helps me understand; He restores the meaning of real truth.

Jim: Are there some things you do, or that He does, which help you on a daily basis?

Elizabeth: Yes, there are. I do some things that I hope enable Him to be more of who He is to me.

In fact, I realized a couple of weeks ago, through another multiple, that my choice of music is based on an awareness of how I guard the gates of my mind. I listen only to music that is uplifting and positive, and about reconciliation and praise. That way I put into my mind what I know will, in time, come back out through my mouth and my heart. If God inhabits the praise of His people, and if my task is conformity to Christ, then this is one quick way to pursue my own healing. Through the renewing of my mind and the transformation of my person by listening to praise on a day-in, day-out basis, I guard the gates of my mind, and miracles happen.

Now this may raise a few eyebrows, but still, when I say, "Let's all pray," it's an ecumenical delight! The "Patty and the Fundamentalettes-for-a-Healing-and-Squealing-Good-Time-for-Jesus" get down on their knees, throw their hands up in the air, squawk in tongues, sing in the spirit, and all that good stuff! The ones who are mainline tend to sit quietly in the pews, and the ones who hang out in the convent run laps around the rosary and meditate. Those who are *still* sitting on the fence saying, "I don't know about this Christian stuff," at least visualize and go along with the values. They're willing to be open because of the way the internal evangelization process goes. The agnostics will try, although they doubt anything will happen. The atheists get on the prayer line, and don't get an answer. It's an ecumenical community!

What I believe is this: When I model what Christ modeled, which is not thumping people over the head with Scriptures every day, then even the agnostics are bound to come along in time.

This is key for all Christians, especially for those who are multiples: Heaven is the result. That's where you end up. Everybody wants to be there but nobody wants to get there! It's the process of learning how to live out "Thou shalt love the Lord thy God with all thy heart and soul" and "Thou shalt have no other

Gods before Me" internally or externally, and "Thou shalt love thy neighbor as thyself" internally and externally. Every alter is as important to me as I am, and if I help them see that importance to each other, how can the hope of salvation be far behind?

Jim: The process of love just scoots its way through all the potential dissention. There *is* no dissention then. With that kind of peace and cooperation, healing will come.

Elizabeth: There is no resistance. You can't have conflict when there is no resistance, so we are just information-seeking, so good choices can be made. And when you look at decision-making, you have to consider the people who will be affected by the choice: Who needs to be informed? Who needs to be responsible? Who needs to approve it? What level of involvement does each one need with this choice?

A 4-year-old obviously needs to be informed if we are going to the circus. If she has an issue about anything connected with the circus, we might need to approve and support her. If it really bugs her, she can back up. When it comes to driving the car, the 4-year-old doesn't need to be responsible. Of those over 16, who is available? Who can go in that direction? Who can handle the trip? So you base your decisions and your choices on fact.

I know that sounds like I'm saying, "Forget feeling." Well, I'm not. Because of the physiology of emotion, most multiples get so caught up in feelings, they forget fact. Nobody teaches them to think logically. That is the basis of process management for me.

Jim: I sense you are pretty much "out there"; you're almost audacious at times . . .

Elizabeth: Absolutely.

Jim: And pretty effective. When you make a presentation and you happen to mention that you are a complex multiple, how do people react to you?

Elizabeth: I have had very little negative backlash. I think when I was first diagnosed, I went through the usual "vanishing friend" syndrome. The management of spoiled identity, which is what the stigma is all about, is a process of beginning to identify how people are going to respond to me, and what I can do to minimize that impact.

Now I get consistently good reviews. When you see someone who's not frothing at the mouth or hurting people right and left, who doesn't run from chair to chair with changing voices, and who acts like a real live human being, it's difficult to pass a lot of judgment.

I don't mean to be tacky, but my one-person-business income tax return might be close to six figures. I'm listed in the 1991 edition of "Who's Who in American Women"; "Who's Who in Finance and Industry"; and, "Who's Who in Emerging Leaders." I am known. I have always been considered brilliant and eccentric, and now we simply know what the eccentricity is!

It's somewhat like the early feminist movement. We used to hear that you don't have to be any better than men to prove anything—you just had to do twice as much. Here is where management of the stigma comes in. I find that if I can consistently excel and consistently produce, if I am transparent about what is going on, and if I get the respect and cooperation from the internal system so I can get the respect and cooperation of the external system, the stigma subsides. People need to be educated. They are afraid of what they don't understand.

One time I was presenting MPD for a psychiatric nursing class meeting at a mental health institute—and nobody came to lock me up! I must not have had a big sign on. The people were amazed. These were just college kids, and what they expected was exactly what they had seen on TV, and exactly what even *current* textbooks had told them multiples are like.

And you know, Jim, if you listen to tapes from conferences, what clinicians say about multiples! You hear blanket pejorative statements about how multiples are resistant and hard to treat, uncooperative and difficult to manage. With all due respect to the people who are in the field, I must say the mindset of the clinicians makes the problem—they do not train the clients. That is as responsible for the treatment difficulties as anything inherent in the disorder itself.

Jim: I completely agree. That is one important part of this book's message. They are wonderful people, and if you give them half a chance, they will work with you.

Elizabeth: Sure! There is no such thing as a resistant client, only a resistant therapist! [Both have a good laugh.] I had a look at a handbook of clinical psychology, *just off the press* in '91—ninety one!—and there's just one single paragraph on dissociative disorders. It relates how rare they are, and how sick those people are. *Nothing else!* This reference book states: "No known studies of incidence to date." These guys didn't do their homework! Today I was listening to a tape from an international conference. It was on working with multiples in an in-patient setting, and again, every single clinician presenting from major dissociative disorder treatment units made disparaging comments about the difficulty of working with multiples.

If I am willing to get my group together, ask what the boundaries are and what they need to be, discuss the risks and what we want to do, and keep working with the process and with the facts, there is no difficulty. "Resistance" cannot continue to exist. This is separate from the abreactive process. It does not replace that process, but it creates a healthy framework for it. As a business consultant, I learned that this is the kind of management it takes. It does not fit a pathology-based process, but clinicians could teach it to their people, and that certainly would speed it up.

Jim: When you talked about therapists, even prominent ones, making disparaging comments about multiples, you made an important observation. A gray cloud seems to hang over this field. The therapists give a subtle message to their clients that they are expected to stop living until they are finished with therapy.

Elizabeth: I think that is pretty much so. Look at the media. Recent segments about multiples on "L. A. Law," "Equal Justice," "Nightline" and "Twenty Four Hours" give you the message that life stops when you are a multiple. We multiples just don't get any social programming indicating that it is possible—*just possible*—that things could be any other way.

Jim: One thing strikes me about that cloud. When the therapist says, "Stop living until we are done with therapy," he's actually training the client to dissociate—to stop living.

Elizabeth: It's a philosophical question. Some therapists are thinking about "functional dissociation." It's very important to be able to use dissociation properly. Every person dissociates. People move away from feelings in certain situations in order to stay in control; otherwise they would go berserk. What we multiples need to learn is how to be *associated*. Not how to dissociate less, but how to remain more associated under more circumstances.

When I go to the doctor I *need* to dissociate effectively, because I'm phobic of doctors. I need to stay associated in my mind and behavior, but it's healthy for me to be somewhat dissociated from my feelings while still in touch with my self. If I didn't, my fear and anxiety would run my blood pressure up to stroke level! In our Western mindset, though, we look at dissociation and say it's bad, and we forget we should be seeking what we want, which is *association*. We need to stay connected to our self in terms of our will, our mind, our emotions, our knowledge and our behavior, connecting them together better and better in our daily life.

Jim: Jesus said that we are not to dissociate from today, by worrying about tomorrow. He said each day has problems of its own, and we are to be attending to each day's problems.

Elizabeth: That is the heart of Jesus' message—life is more than just following rules. Jesus' focus was on love. We need to learn to stay associated at all those levels—and live each day out through the process of love.

Jim: In my first book I emphasized having the multiple stay in his (or her) daily routine while in therapy if it is possible. I want multiples to learn how to use dissociation for their benefit. That means keeping the more mature selves running the daily routine, and negotiating with the ones who need healing, so they will wait for a better time to get that healing. The systems need to be given lessons on how to stay as functional as possible. I stand with that approach.

Elizabeth: I stand with it also, Jim. It is critical, and that is why I don't believe in hospitalization. If you get out of your daily routine, you begin in subtle ways to reward failure. We all need to see the rewards for staying functional.

One time, when I was living in a lovely, 1100-square-foot apartment with a waterfall in the front yard, driving a new car, and traveling whenever I wanted to—I was enjoying the benefits of feeling good—I said to my group, "Hey guys. Do you like the house? Do you like the car? Do you like being able to take a vacation now and then? Do you like having somebody do the housecleaning, since nobody likes to clean house?"

The answer was "Yeah!"

I said, "Okay. No problem! Let's figure out how to keep working."

Jim: So those are the benefits. You can keep on living.

Elizabeth: You can have self-respect, self-esteem. You have the benefit of self-discipline instead of self-abuse. You don't have to go on disability, or become a burden to anyone, not even yourself. Your self-love is a lot higher—it's based on respect and esteem.

Jim: You know, it just occurred to me that, if a person is waiting to live until therapy is over, that person will have no joy. The idea of "joy" is living. You want to *associate* joy with the successes of working on each day's problems. You can't be in the middle of enjoyment if you're waiting to get healthy.

Elizabeth: Absolutely. Here's one of the ways I began training myself to do that, six or seven years ago, and I didn't even know I was doing it at the time. I could remember the times when I felt mad and could recreate the feeling in a few seconds, but I could not remember when I felt joyful. I also had figured out that happiness is an effect—a short term effect in the middle of a bunch of effects, on the way to a result. The result was joy. I said, "What are the emotional results I would like to see in my life? Victory, peace, joy, harmony, gentleness, patience and freedom." Then I said "I've got to have change. Everybody has to have change. You might as well create it."

So I took those seven emotional qualities, and I coupled them with the seven days of the week, and I assigned colors to them. Monday was "victory" and the color was violet. I knew I could remember a time in my life when I was victorious, not where somebody else lost, but where everybody won. For example, I'd ask myself, "Do you remember when you were trying to ride your bike, and all of a sudden you could do it all by yourself, and your dad and your brother didn't have to push you any more? That was a victory for us all."

I began on a daily basis to put up a library within myself of times I felt victory, or peace, or all seven categories. I had cards stuck here and there that asked, "What are you feeling?" Well I feel anxious. "What do you want to feel?" If it was Monday, I wanted to feel victory. "Okay, stop and remember a time in your life when you felt victory." I would turn it up, like I would turn up the volume on a radio. When I had it fully in my whole body, then I'd look around and give thanks for it. Then I'd look at all the violet things around, and begin to get a triple association. Monday—victory—violet.

I did that five or six times a day, and I stuck with the "feeling *du jour,*" for a couple of years. I found that in general I was a more cheerful person. I saw the wins in my life more readily. It changed my life.

Jim: You were *associating* with the feelings, and trying to control the levels at which you were feeling them.

Elizabeth: Right. And now when I use that process—I call it the victory cycle—I begin using the strength to associate with what I want and get some control through choice, every day. The alters can choose to do it. It can be a form of praising God. If you pick out the fruits of the spirit for the seven days—love, joy, peace, patience, faith, goodness, and self-control—then you are focusing on the "fruits" of the spirit.

Jim: So you're guarding your gates, and bringing in the things that God has laid out for you.

Elizabeth: And you're allowing your mind to be transformed and renewed, and you're focusing on things that are good and wholesome.

Jim: I really like that process. Yesterday I was leading a seminar, and somebody asked the question, "Does everybody need integration?" I said focusing on integration was a sidetrack. You focus on healing.

Elizabeth: Right. If you focus on healing, which is a process, God's results will follow.

Jim: If you stay with letting God transform your mind through these seven fruits of the spirit, the results will come about.

Elizabeth: You have to reassociate with your will—be willing to participate in letting God do it. I am as responsible for my part of allowing my mind to be transformed as God is for His part. If God's knocking, and I won't let Him in because I'm not willing to, then He isn't transforming me. A lot of alters think that if I turn my will over to Him, I will come out a rabid "jerk for Jesus." That's not at all true. It's not becoming a "you're going to hell and I'm not" person. Alters desperately need to hear this message. It's not an offer of religious abuse or of dysfunctional faith, but of what it really means to be a person of God—a compassionate, strong, standing-still, gentle, patient person of God, unable to abuse others.

Jim: As I view the process of dissociation,* I believe the will is the weakest link—the first thing to split off. The least amount of tension will split a person at the level of the will. So if the battle is won at the *will* level—if you have *associated* the will of the alters to be transformed by God, you have the most certainty of co-operation.

Elizabeth: Absolutely. Absolutely. One of the quotes I use in my workbook is: "Live your life from love instead of hate. If you must have revenge, remember that the sweetest revenge is successful living." When you are known to be a multiple, people expect you to be so far removed from successful living that successful living is, in fact, very sweet.

---

*   For a more extensive discussion, see *Uncovering the Mystery of MPD,* chapter 4.

13

MERIBETH:
Turning
the Corner

LAST WEEK I saw an old friend at a gas station. He does not live nearby, so our chance encounter really caught me by surprise.

I called to him across the lot, "Steve, why have we met here today?"

He whirled around, and began laughing before he said anything. "Do you think we have been put here for some cosmic reason?" he retorted.

"Evidently."

We talked for a few minutes, and I found he is writing a book, too. He told me a few things about it and had a few questions that I could help him with. He said he has been hearing good things about my first book, so I told him I was putting together another one. He was interested. I took the proposed table of contents out of my briefcase and showed it to him. He told me we are in perfect agreement about how marvelous multiples are, and he asked if I was still looking for people to interview. When I said it is not too late, he suggested I telephone his friend, Meribeth. He has kept in touch with her for about seven years, long after she was discharged from the mental hospital where they had met.

Steve said without reservation that Meribeth is a splendid person. He had worked with her when she was a patient. She had been completely unmanageable at times—it could take the whole male staff to get her quieted down—yet she won everyone's heart. She eventually came to the point, after many setbacks, where she simply determined she would get healthy, and she stuck with her decision. She had gotten some help from Christianity during her recovery, which helped her turn the corner to health. I knew I should talk with her. She recently moved half a continent away but he said he would give her a call and get back to me.

I looked down and spotted two pennies on the pavement, a few feet from where we were standing. Pointing to them, I told Steve we could each have a lucky penny, but that was probably not the cosmic reason we met. The pennies were both scratched up and battered, but we had another good laugh and each picked one up.

The next day Steve called and gave me Meribeth's phone number. After only a few minutes on the telephone with her, it seemed we were old friends. Our mutual connection with Steve put her entirely at ease with me. She had not heard of my other book, so she did not really know the kind of things I might be asking about. Her life is still being restored, and her story is one of pain and progress, of despair and tenacity. Maybe most important of all, it is a story of how faith came to a person who asked for it, and how that faith meant survival.

* * *

Jim: Steve told me what a great friend you are, and he mentioned you were in and out of the hospital a lot. That would be a good place to start our discussion.

Meribeth: I had been in the hospital a long time before Steve started working there. I was a "well-known" patient, being a multiple personality. Some of my personalities were pretty disruptive. They had to be restrained part of the time.

Jim: Why would they have to be restrained?

Meribeth: At the time, two of them were out of control. One was coming out, trying to escape. She would take off and run, and try to break out of doors—and this was a locked facility. Another personality was a male. He tried to protect her and attacked the staff. So it would end up a big take-down, with almost every staff member involved. I'd get seclusion and isolation, and major amounts of Thorazine. That would happen a couple of times a week. But it only happened while I was in hospitals—never in public.

Jim: It is important to me that they knew you had the diagnosis of multiplicity, so they should have been concerned with getting you to switch back into non-aggressive personalities. Restraining should have been brief, and the staff should have befriended the one who wanted to escape and helped her to know she was safe. She must have been extremely fearful.

Meribeth: It took a while to convince the staff about the MPD. My doctor had it written down on the chart, but the staff would not go for it. Back then it was taboo. Multiple personalities did not exist. They thought people were just putting on acts and it was treated poorly. Patients who had it were called schizophrenic and were put on drugs. I was diagnosed schizophrenic for a long time and was given large amounts of drugs I shouldn't have been on.

Jim: That would make it almost impossible for you to operate. The way I understand it, antipsychotic medications just slow your whole nervous system down, and only one or two of your personalities are able to get out at all.

Meribeth: Right. It was a nightmare. I thought of myself as one personality, but then I found I had these other personalities, plus being locked up, plus having to fight staff!

Jim: So you believed the MPD diagnosis, but the staff didn't, except your doctor?

Meribeth: Right. At first my doctor put it in the chart just because he had to put something down, but I don't think he truly believed it then. He didn't know how to work with it. He never tried to learn about it. He just medicated me.

But I found some staff people who were willing to work with me. That was the only time I was able to find out what was going on with the blackouts, the different personalities. It wasn't through my doctor but through a couple of staff members I happened to be working with. I have read that if you don't *have* to, don't put a multiple in a locked ward. Too many staff people tell the patient that MPD is not what they have; that it's her imagination; that she's making it up; and they do not give the personalities any validity. Then the personalities won't come out. They won't work. They act up.

Jim: So hospitalization made things quite a bit worse than they were on the outside?

Meribeth: Yes. The reason I would be put into the hospital was that I would get strongly suicidal. One of my personalities was very suicidal. Those were times I needed to be in the hospital. It kept me alive, but not much else.

Jim: How long would you have to stay, after being admitted for suicidality?

Meribeth: First it was for a year.

Jim: A whole year?

Meribeth: The second time it was another year, at a different hospital. Then after that, it would be a month or a few months. Whatever the insurance would cover.

Jim: And when the insurance ran out, so would you?

Meribeth: I would have to leave for a certain amount of time, but I would end up coming back in.

Jim: Did you want to be hospitalized?

Meribeth: I believed it was the best for me. With all the splitting, I didn't know how to survive on the outside. So it was safer in the hospital, even though it caused the personalities to act out all the more. I thought that was where I belonged, actually. I thought I was going to be in the hospital the rest of my life!

Jim: Did you develop a personality to stay there?

Meribeth: Yes. That was the bad part about putting somebody in for a year. You get to know hospital life, but that's all you know. That becomes your world. You learn how to live in it, and you learn to know the staff. It's a safe environment.

Jim: I'd bet it was safer than whatever was making you suicidal. So now, here you are years later, leading a domestic life.

How did you get on the correct path to health, since it wasn't coming from the hospital?

Meribeth: I finally switched doctors. The treatment I got from the doctor I had at the time was unhealthy for me. He had decided I was too much trouble, but that turned out to be a good thing for me. I started to see another doctor, a therapist from the same hospital. He worked well with me and with the personalities. He was the first person I trusted to work with the personalities. Most of the time, it had been almost like I was in a circus, like I was performing for people. I didn't feel they were trying to help me—it was more, "Well, let's see if she really does it." And that made the personalities stop coming out.

This doctor started helping me get control back for the emotions I had dissociated. With his help, during the next five years I learned how to accept the emotions—the rage, the anger, the hate—and I learned that these feelings were okay.

Jim: It sounds like your personalities made the choice to deal with feelings. Some people have personalities that will do anything they can to stay away from feelings. They try to get through therapy without dealing with feelings. They want to stay on the intellectual level, but it sounds like you had encouragement and the tenacity to work with the nasty feelings.

Meribeth: Yes. I knew that if I was going to have a functioning life, I couldn't throw away the difficult feelings. Not that they're bad, the anger and the rage and the hurt and all that—but I have to compromise with all the personalities.

Jim: So it's more of a team situation for your system?

Meribeth: Yes, mostly. I've still got some problems, but I've learned how to avoid them, and to keep out of situations that would cause me to split or to lose time. The other day I talked to somebody who knows I have this, and I told him I can't be around people who might go into a rage in front of me. I still can't deal with that. I'll split and remove myself, and one of the personalities will come out and take over. Then I'll lose time.

Jim: You were in out-patient treatment for about five years? During that time, was there some merging of personalities, or a decision not to merge?

Meribeth: I don't think any of them merged. They just got closer to me. I got to know them, and I quit denying that they existed. I used to get angry when these personalities would come out and take time away from me. They would have memories of what I did, but I would have no memories of what they did. I would get angry and scared. Other people would like these personalities, and I didn't like that. So I had to work through it.

Jim: Eventually you all became friends?

Meribeth: I don't know that we became friends. We work together. I still have one who is suicidal. It is more of a team effort. They work it out on the inside.

Jim: What helped you most?

Meribeth: I had to deal with the fact that I was an alcoholic. One of the worst things a multiple can do is drink. It causes the splitting to be even more severe. That was happening a lot in hospitals.

Jim: You would drink in hospitals?

Meribeth: I would go out on a pass and come back drunk. I came to the decision that I had to stop drinking. That happened three years ago, and it's really helped. I started to get my confidence back and I started to realize that I am a good person, not this weird, crazy person I had been led to believe I was.

Jim: So when you quit drinking, the system worked together better?

Meribeth: Yes. Alcohol affects the different personalities differently. It's the same with the major drugs they put people on in hospitals. The medication would affect the personalities differently.

Jim: Some of the personalities would be wiped out by the Thorazine and others would be unaffected?

Meribeth: Yes, and others would have bad reactions to it. It was crazy. With the alcohol, some of the personalities would get drunk and some wouldn't, some are kids, some are adults. It affects each of them in different ways. It was chaotic. Just for my own self, I had to quit drinking. Since then, I haven't lost much time. I still need therapy. I was in therapy in California, and now that I've moved out here, I need to get back to working on the issues I still need to deal with. It's a daily struggle not to run away from feelings, not to stuff them. I need to keep that in mind every day, or relapse will occur. The structure will break down.

Jim: Have you had any relapses?

Meribeth: No, I haven't. My dad died recently, and I had a breakdown, but I didn't lose any time. I had to be hospitalized because I was so depressed.

Jim: The suicidal personalities weren't coming out?

Meribeth: No.

Jim: That is a good sign.

Meribeth: As long as I let myself feel the feelings, then I'm doing what I told them I would do: I will feel the feelings. I will not run away from them.

Jim: So you let their feelings come to you, and you don't minimize them and turn them away?

Meribeth: That's right. I don't disregard the personalities any more. I accept them as being part of my life, that they are real, and that's fine. And I don't get angry with them any more.

Jim: That sounds workable.

Meribeth: It is workable for me. It is really up to the individual with MPD, whether she wants to go for full integration, or whether it is better to work as a team. Some people need to feel whole in order to function, to feel like a real person. Others don't want to give up the personalities. They think they can work together. It seems to work for them. It's an individual thing. Not everybody has to integrate.

Jim: I guess each person has to decide how he or she is going to live life. If some want to live it the way you are, that is their choice.

Meribeth: Maybe later I will integrate. Down the road I may need to, but for now, it works, and I'm for anything that works, anything that lets me function on a daily basis.

Jim: Was there any kind of a spiritual dimension to your therapy that propelled you along toward health, or maybe even away from health, for that matter?

Meribeth: I had been brought up with a strong sense that there is a God, and it was a good upbringing. I had a spiritual sense, but I wasn't in touch with it. While I was in the hospital, I sort of got into the satanic part of it. That really caused problems.

Jim: In the hospital?

Meribeth: While I was in there I had gotten some books on satanic worship. It really took me in. It seemed a quick way of feeling good. All I wanted to do was to feel good and not to lose time. These books proclaimed that you would feel good and that wonderful things would happen, but it caused problems.

Jim: Did you get into Satan worship?

Meribeth: In a way I did. I started to follow the books. They took me in that this was satanic, but it was a natural earth kind of thing. It took me in fast. I knew things were going bad for me as I read those books, so I started to pray a lot. That seemed to help and I got away from it.

Jim: Was this all by yourself, or did you have to join a group of people?

Meribeth: All alone. It's amazing how these books can get you going. If I hadn't been in the hospital for that year, it would have been easy for me to get in with people like that. The books claim that life would be wonderful. It took everything the Bible said and twisted it. For somebody who is hurting and is trying to find something that will work quickly, that would seem the way to go.

Jim: It sounds innocent enough, and kind of unthreatening, just to pick up a book and read it.

Meribeth: But you start believing in Satan and following his way. The book had incantations and things like that. When you start praying that way, it starts growing in your mind.

Jim: Do you think there was any evidence of evil spirits?

Meribeth: I do. I really do. I went through a hard time when I got angry at God and turned away. Things happened too quickly for evil spirits not to be some kind of an influence. The belief that dying was the best way to go became strong when I got into these books. It was weird.

It wasn't until later, when I started to get back into God, that I noticed the evil influence. There was one suicide attempt when I tried to jump off a building. It didn't feel like me; it seemed something else was telling me to do this. It wasn't my decision—it was a feeling of total despair. I was in a dark hole, and just before I was ready to jump, I said, "God, I need help." Immediately a lifting, a kind of lightness, and tremendously good feeling came into me. I was grabbed off the building by a staff person, and things started falling into place. So I am convinced that merely getting into the books—I've talked to teenagers about this and about not getting involved with groups—it can change you. The books and groups are that strong.

Jim: That is a good warning. Was "getting into God" picking up a Bible and getting into that book?

Meribeth: No, it was more praying and talking to others who were firm believers, and associating with them. I could see their faith in their lives. They were happy and free inside.

Jim: When you were changing over to God, was that shortly after the "top of the building" episode?

Meribeth: Yes, it was. Getting back was a slow process, but I had a pretty good foundation after I asked for help. People with strong spirituality came into my life after that. Suddenly they were just around me and were there to help me.

Jim: When you asked God for help, and felt the lightness, do you think it was a kind of exorcism, or something like that?

Meribeth: It was like breaking inner bonds. I was weighed down and hadn't noticed it at the time. I was tied—I didn't have any freedom. But I could certainly feel the release inside.

Jim: Were the spiritual people who would come to your aid from the hospital?

Meribeth: Yes. The security guard happened to come by and see me, and he would relay his beliefs in God. Then he came to see me twice a week with his daughter. People came from places I wouldn't expect; for example, a nurse who had strong spiritual beliefs suddenly took an interest in me. I hadn't exactly asked for people, but they came to me because I had simply prayed.

Jim: It must have hit you strongly that God must be on your side.

Meribeth: It did. It helped me start to see that there was hope, where I thought before there was none. I began to realize I was a worthwhile person and I could work through whatever it was I had to deal with. I knew it would be a long process, but I also knew that, as long as I kept in touch with God and kept a strong belief, I would make it. That has kept me alive and has helped me be where I am today.

Jim: How long did it take, after you were spiritually freed, until you were unhospitalized and on your own?

Meribeth: For about five more years I was in and out of the hospital, and I got a new doctor.

Jim: Was the new doctor more spiritually attuned than the other one, or wasn't that a factor?

Meribeth: I think it was. I could see right away that he was a caring individual. He really cared about what I had been going through—it wasn't just the money aspect. Under him, I felt I could be successful with some guidance, and he was willing to stick with me. He was a lot different from the first doctor. I did ask him if he believed in God, and he said he did, but it was not something we talked about much; I just could sense it in him.

Jim: Over that long a course of treatment, you must have hit pockets of despair now and then. How did you deal with them?

Meribeth: I prayed, and I knew, somewhere in there, that some day what I needed would happen. I had a strong faith. Even the times I did give up, God never did. When I would get low, a sense would come to me, not *from* me, but from somewhere would come this sense that I would be okay.

Jim: How did God comfort you or help you?

Meribeth: I don't know how to explain it exactly. I would hear something in my head, and I would just get an inner peace, a real calming of my insides, where I had been worried and panicked before. I would just know, suddenly, that it was going to be okay, and I knew was God comforting me inside.

Jim: Before we stop, is there anything else you'd like to talk about?

Meribeth: Yes. I am so concerned for people who get hospitalized, and get misdiagnosed, and get drugged for acting out. It can be a nightmare.

Jim: Well, there are a few hospitals that specialize in working with MPD now—they work with nothing but that. However, I believe that in many hospitals, people with MPD still come in and get a lot of attention for their dividedness instead of their splendidness. They are not encouraged to grow into their best self. Often the staff is more interested in reporting to their friends about the MPD than they are in learning to work with it more effectively.

Meribeth: I know. I got tired of saying, "This is real. Please help me." But I always seemed to find people who genuinely cared, even in hospitals. I hope that will be the case for others, but I am concerned that so many multiples are not getting the right kind of hospital care, and a multiple can get stuck there. That doesn't have to happen anymore. There just needs to be a lot of education.

14

KELTIE:
Trampling
the Serpent

WHILE TALKING with a therapist at a conference, I learned of a recovered multiple who is another one of those "splendid people." Keltie, who refers to herself as an "overcomer," helps people understand more about abuse by speaking to small groups. This encourages survivors to start dealing with their own abuse. Rosie, her therapist, told me that in addition to the speaking, Keltie does volunteer work tirelessly, is helping rewrite the counseling center's procedures, leads children's Bible study groups at her church, and composes poetry in her spare time. There was such a lilt in Rosie's voice as she talked, I knew I had to ask Keltie if she would contribute her story to this book. Here it is.

Jim: What first put you in touch with the memories of your abuse?

Keltie: The initial return of the memory shocked me. At my father's place, a very large turtle walked across the yard toward a fishpond my father had dug and stocked. He didn't want the turtle in there because it would eat the fish. So he went outside, and when I saw him go around the house to get his axe, I realized he was going to kill the turtle. I tried to stop him but couldn't get the door open fast enough. I saw him kill the turtle with the axe.

That brought back memories of the abuse, because I had at one time decided to kill my abuser with that same axe. My father had used it to kill chickens on the farm where I was raised, so I knew it was an instrument of death. I was a child, and I needed something to stop what was happening, and that's what I chose to use. I had asked God to stop the abuse, even though I feared God terribly, but I was desperate. When God didn't kill my abuser, I decided I had to do it. Shortly after that, my abuser died of a heart attack. I concluded that God had killed him because of my request, and I was therefore the murderer. That's why I dissociated the memories—I couldn't live with myself. They didn't return until this incident, which took place when I was in my 40s.

Jim: How did the killing of the turtle awaken the memory?

Keltie: All I remember at this point is screaming and running away. I ran to my house, and my roommate asked me what was wrong, because I was obviously hysterical. I told her a murder had been committed. Of course, she was upset, but when I finally managed to explain to her what I had seen, she told me you don't use the word *murder* if it's a turtle. You use the word *kill.*

That night, when I tried to sleep, I experienced the return of a recurring childhood dream, and I started to remember the abuse. I didn't remember it all at once. I compare the return of the memory with an archeological dig—it only comes back a little at a time. The first memories were about the sexual abuse I suffered between the ages of 6 and 10. Later I began to remember the more sadistic things that occurred with the ritual abuse during the years I was 8 to 10. Then in therapy I was able to recall some earlier ritual abuse.

Jim: Is that where the word *murder* came from?

Keltie: No. I believe it came from my wanting to kill my abuser. I had planned to kill him with the axe, and I never quite separated that thought from the way he died. I never really believed he died of a heart attack. I believed I had killed him.

Jim: When you did begin to archaeologically uncover this series of memories, had you been in treatment already, or did you start seeking treatment shortly after that?

Keltie: No, I went through about a six-month period when I had flashbacks and nightmares and incidents during which I disappeared but didn't know where I'd been. I'd find myself someplace, not knowing how I'd gotten there. I realized I was bouncing off the wall—something was terribly wrong. At that point someone advised me to seek counseling, but I refused because I was afraid. Some time after that I heard an announcement on the radio for a seminar at the Christian counseling center, for adult victims of child sexual abuse. I thought a seminar was non-threatening, and perhaps I could learn to forget all this. I went to the seminar, and of course they did not teach me how to forget it. In fact, they wanted me to remember it, walk through it, and remove the threat that it was to me.

Jim: How much did that take place during the seminar time?

Keltie: Not very much, but Rosie, the center's director, recognized I had a serious problem and needed help. She was able to talk with me, and she convinced me to at least attend one group session. That session was the first time I had disclosed to anyone what had happened. I gave a very brief description of the part of the abuse that I remembered—and then I passed out!

Jim: You mean you were flat on the floor?

Keltie: Yes. I woke up on the floor!

Jim: Oh, my!

Keltie: People were caring for me. That's when Rosie convinced me I needed to come back because I couldn't take the chance of this happening on my job, at home or in the car.

Jim: What made you pass out?

Keltie: I believe it was the tension. I was trying so hard not to show any emotion, holding everything in, trying to go through the steps that I believed were expected of me. I'd simply reveal what had happened, and then go home.

Jim: Hoping it would be that simple.

Keltie: I had very little understanding of what was ahead for me. It's a good thing I didn't know, because I probably would have run. That was my way of coping with problems.

Jim: But this time the group cared enough about you to ask you to be part of them, and they wouldn't let you run?

Keltie: Rosie wouldn't let me run. The others didn't know me, but they were very caring. They gave me their phone numbers to call if I needed support. That impressed me. I had been a Christian for ten years by then, but I hadn't understood Christian love—unconditional love. I had a confused idea of what love was all about. One of the things my abuser did was to tell me he loved me, and then he would do hurtful things to me.

Jim: That will twist things, won't it? So how did it go for you early in treatment?

Keltie: It was very difficult because I was unable to talk about it. I wanted to comply with Rosie, to be obedient. I knew I wanted healing, and I knew she knew how to get it for me. But I just couldn't talk.

We discovered during the therapy that a curse had been pronounced over me: If I ever told anyone what the ritual abusers were doing to me, I would have to kill the person I told, and then I would have to kill myself. By the time I went into individual therapy with Rosie, I had developed enough of a relationship with her, that I didn't want to hurt her. I wasn't consciously aware I would have to, but inside of me I knew that if I opened my mouth, I would have to kill her, and then kill myself. I was too uncomfortable to talk. We would spend long therapy sessions with only a few words exchanged.

Jim: And all that time you had the knowledge of what you wanted to say, but you just couldn't say it?

Keltie: The knowledge came back gradually. As it started out, I had only the memory of the sexual abuse. The other memories came later. I believe the Lord only gave me what I could tolerate at any one time.

A friend of my father began to abuse me when I was six. My father was also taking pornographic pictures of me, and he gave me to this man. At one point my brother became involved. At another, I realized my mother was aware of it. The sexual abuse started that way, but my father later became involved with some cult members, and that's where the ritual abuse came in. The character of the abuse changed radically at that point. Through physical, mental and emotional torments, I was conditioned to be obedient. The tactics were similar to those used on prisoners of war.

Jim: And as these memories came back, you found it impossible to talk?

Keltie: I would try to lead the conversation somewhere else.

Jim: So how did you break through that? What helped you to finally open up and talk freely?

Keltie: I withdrew into what we later discovered was my escape personality, and Rosie would talk to her. She uncovered information about a ritual in which I was given to Astareth and Incubus at my grandfather's home, before I was 2. Rosie prayed that the Lord would reveal to her what curses were spoken over me. By that time the Lord had revealed to Rosie that there were also other personalities involved. The personalities were developed in my childhood because I was not allowed to express any kind of feelings. I had nowhere to go with the anger, so I created an angry personality who could go into the closet when nobody was there and beat on the clothing, and just be in a rage.

At one point in my counseling, this personality tried to attack Rosie but was prevented from it. Apparently—I know this sounds strange—that personality *saw* some men in the room and she later identified them as angels. They held her back, and poked at her if she became abusive to Rosie. During that encounter Rosie discovered there had been a curse to harm anyone who was told about the abuse. That personality was the only violent one, so that's the one who would have to do the killing. Rosie broke the curse, and that personality began to open up and talk.

I created one personality to take my anger and rage, and I created another personality to take me away from danger, and I created a third personality who would receive the pain and fear so I could remain emotionless. That personality never grew; it remained an 8-year-old child. When she was first contacted, and asked for her name, she simply said, "I'm nobody."

Jim: What happened to her?

Keltie: She finally chose a name for herself, and Rosie introduced her to the Lord and worked very hard with her. She was the one most wounded. She believed she had been skinned alive, and Rosie prayed for God to heal her. She told Rosie that Jesus put her skin back on. Eventually, there was a fusion, but it took a year after the fusion took place to nurture that personality. Rosie had to work through me and my other alters to help her. Rosie also prayed for the angels to come to her and help her, and one of the other alters read the Bible and some Bible story books Rosie provided. I feel now that she has grown quite strong, and is fully a part of me.

Jim: How long into treatment was it when you found you had multiple personality?

Keltie: I didn't find out until about two years into it. My reaction was extreme anger. I refused to accept it. I put up my fists and began beating on Rosie, blaming her, and telling her she was lying to me. I followed that by going into my angry personality and just raging. I wrote lots of poetry in fierce anger about it, and I raged toward the first personality Rosie said I had, which was the escape personality. Something happened at a seminar I attended. The escape personality came out and was recognized by another person who had multiple personalities. So she went to Rosie and said, "Somebody is living inside of Keltie."

Rosie came and talked to me, and realized it was true. She made contact with the escape personality, the only one who knew everybody else. I never developed more than three personalities—one for escape, one for anger, and one for pain and fear. The fear personality was about 8 years old, the escape personality apparently grew into a young woman—she started out as a child—and the anger personality was a teenager.

Jim: How long did the therapy go on for you?

Keltie: About four years.

Jim: After the three personalities had become joined with you, what did it feel like?

Keltie: It was an immediate euphoria. I was overwhelmed, I was overjoyed, I felt whole for the first time. I thought at that time, "It's over. I'm healed. Everything's okay. I'm never going to have any more problems." But then I began to realize that healing is a process and not an event. I understood, after a while, that I had to continue to work with it. Although I was back together and feeling everything all in one place, I was not accustomed to it and the first time I felt emotional pain, I thought I would die. I had to learn how to use my new wholeness to face problems. I suppose, if I would not stay in the Lord and remain faithful to what I have learned, I could slip back to old habits and run away from things. That's my inclination whenever something difficult comes at me. But now I am able to stand up to things, because I'm whole and I've learned how to use that to my advantage.

One difficult thing was a confrontation with my family. They had dominated me almost all my life. I was totally unable to break away from them. As I look back now, I can see that the Lord prepared me carefully and brought me to the day when the confrontation took place.

At that point, I remember consciously deciding to go with the Lord toward freedom. I remember thinking, *The Lord has prepared me for this. He wants me to be free. He wants me to be healed. I'm afraid, but that's what I have to do.* I knew the alternative was to be enslaved by my family for the rest of my life. So even though I received a beating for it, I stood up to my family. I left the home I was in at the time; I was given a safe house to stay in; and I did not let my family know where I was. When I contacted them again, I told them there would be boundaries. I use this as a pattern for any kind of problems that come up now, instead of running away from them.

Jim: Are you saying that all your life you have lived with your family, and only when you got whole, you were able to move away?

Keltie: That's right. But I'm not taking the credit. I believe the Lord set the opportunity before me. If He hadn't, I don't know whether I'd have gone for it on my own.

Jim: Until then, they could trigger you, and you would escape and not confront them—you could not stand up to them?

Keltie: That's correct. They told me what to do, when to do it, where to do it, and why to do it. I obeyed everything. Now I am trying to establish a reasonable relationship with my mother. I'm starting with her. I am setting boundaries for my brothers and sisters, letting them know what they can and cannot do, and what I will and will not put up with.

Jim: A little self-care goes a long way, doesn't it?

Keltie: Yes, indeed.

Jim: That's a wonderful thing!

Keltie: Isn't it? I feel so free! It does wonders for your self-esteem!

Jim: Can you tell me what role God played in this for you?

Keltie: God is the whole thing! I didn't know it at the time, but as I look back, I can see His footprints all over my life. One of the things I asked Rosie in an angry way, at the very beginning of my counseling was, "Where was God when all of this happened?"

She responded, "He was with you," and I said she was lying. But I can see now how He cared for me, how He kept me safe, how He kept me alive, how He removed people who were endangering me at various times, how He waited until I was ready and then came to me in a rebirth experience. He waited until I was ready to say yes to Him. I praise Him for that!

I believe the Lord has work for me to do now, and I have given myself to that, even though what He has for me frightens me. The nature of the work scares me because in my childhood I was not allowed to express any kind of emotions, and I had to withdraw. I eventually became temporarily mute. I couldn't speak at all, and as I grew, I developed a serious phobia about speaking in public. It got to the point where I couldn't even speak to anyone on the telephone without having a terrible panic attack. I certainly couldn't stand in front of an audience. Now the Lord has me speaking to groups of people, especially women, about childhood sexual abuse and ritual abuse, and assuring them there is healing and there is hope. About 25 percent of the people I speak to have something like this in their backgrounds.

One thing that is difficult for me is when this is referred to as "service," because I was called a "servant slave" in the ceremonies, and that terminology still repels me. However, I know the Lord is working with me on this.

Jim: It's pretty awful to realize there are that many people—one in four—who need to remember and to go through what it takes to overcome the sexual abuse trauma.

Keltie: Every time I speak, people tiptoe up to me afterward, and reveal that they are adult survivors of child sexual abuse.

Jim: On the average, how often are you called on to speak like this?

Keltie: It varies. Next month I have at least three speaking engagements set up. It's usually by word of mouth. We don't do any advertising. I got a message on my answering machine tonight, from somebody I don't know, who wants me to call and set up a speaking date.

Jim: Do you have a special way of presenting the material?

Keltie: I usually tell the audience I am going to relate one particular case at our center. I say I am a volunteer there, and that I have permission from the survivor. I talk about the family and dysfunctional problems in the family, and show on a chart how it travels through generations and why it's necessary to break the dysfunctional cycle. Then I tell about the case study, all the way from childhood to adulthood. At the very end of the presentation, I reveal that I am that person. Then I field questions.

Jim: That sounds pretty effective. When you present this to them, what do you say about hope and healing?

Keltie: I assure them that when a child is traumatized the attack is not only on the mental, emotional and physical, but also on the spiritual part of the person. The hope and the healing is in finding a counselor who can deal with the spiritual side. Every part of the person is shattered and broken, and torn apart, and the whole person needs nurturing and care to restore identity. I assure them that I'm not against secular counseling, but I really don't feel full healing is possible if the spiritual part is ignored. I also speak about how important the Lord has been to me, how much He has done for me, how much He loves me, and how my concept of Him has changed. I thought of Him as very angry, judgmental and punishing, like my father was. I feared Him. Long after I became a Christian, I was able to relate with Jesus but I still wasn't able to relate with God the Father. Little by little,

God made Himself known to me as the father I never had. I explain to the group how important it has been for me to have a loving father in God, how healing that has been for me. I tell them God has given me the nurturing my earthly father was unable to give me.

Usually I can see that a lot of people in the audience relate to that. There are always a number of people visibly in pain. Many, many women, especially, have relational problems with their fathers, and it affects their concept of God.

I expressed my pain through therapy in a way I never used before—Rosie asked me to keep a journal. I found it extremely difficult to do because it was so much like having to sit and talk with her. That had always been hard for me. So I wrote 60 or 70 poems, and expressed many of my emotions in that way. I even wrote poetry to my other personalities at the time they were discovered. Some of the poems were angry. As time went on, though, they became much more accepting, even reaching out to nurture the child personalities.

Jim: That is terrific. The poetry became something they accepted as their own because it was a gift.

Keltie: I had the foresight to keep track of the order in which they were written, so I can look back at them now and see the stages of my healing. I can see just when everything happened.

Jim: You said you are a volunteer at the counseling center, and you do some speaking. Are there other things you do as well?

Keltie: Yes, I do administrative assistant type work at the center. I type up things for the director, develop written formats for policies and procedures for the agency, and help raise funds for clients who can't afford to pay for counseling. I also hope to write my own story, and perhaps get something published some-day, so it can be used to help fund programs at the center.

Jim: Are you a writer?

Keltie: I'm praying I am. I never thought of myself as a writer, but Rosie said I had the ability when she saw the poetry in my journal. I had never done any writing before that. Others, too, say I have the ability.

Jim: Evidently. And it started to become noticeable during the therapy time, as the feelings were being made available for your power.

Keltie: I was asked to release them, but I was reluctant to do that. So I tried poetry and found that it was a good medium. It was legal to invent words and I could say things in unusual ways. I could get the feelings out so that I understood them, but nobody except other survivors could really enter in.

Jim: So you spend about how many hours each week at the counseling center?

Keltie: I go there after work every day. I have a full time job, and I spend all my evenings doing one thing or another for the center. I go out on weekends for speaking engagements, and I also do volunteer work at my church.

Jim: What kind of volunteer work?

Keltie: Right now I'm developing a fund-raising program for our building fund. I also teach in the Christian education program, and assist them in any other way I can. I have a very loving church family. I'm the only person in my church I know who has had these kinds of problems, or at least has admitted having them. And I am the only one who has gone through therapy. It's been difficult at times for them because I have had flashbacks, and emotional situations have occurred there as I went through the therapy. But I must say my church family has worked very hard to learn how to deal with somebody like me. They've grown with me, and they fully support all of my volunteer work, even when I can't be in church on Sundays because I'm speaking. They often pray for me. I am also the coordinator of the prayer group at church, and I'm a member of the intercessory prayer group and the Ways and Means Committee at the center.

Jim: I think I'm getting exhausted just listening to your schedule. Were you that busy before you went through therapy?

Keltie: Oh no! All this came about as I was filled with the Lord. I am so greatful to the center and to God for my healing. I just ask the Lord to use me, and boy, does He ever!

Jim: It sounds like it, and you give Him plenty of chances.

Keltie: I'm just thrilled to be able to be used. I'm excited. You know, I can't wait to leave my everyday job, so I can work on the important things they do at the center.

Jim: It sounds like your heart is really in the Lord's work. It seems to have made all the difference in the world to you.

Keltie: Oh, yes. Oh, yes. I wouldn't go back for anything. No way. Life is completely different now, and I owe it to the Lord, and to the fact that the people at the center open themselves to Him, and allow Him to use them.

Let me say just one more thing. I'm *not* glad I was abused, but I *am* glad I have the opportunity to come back at Satan, and try to turn it around. I'm not his victim. Romans 8:28 says it well. God is working in all things for our good.

Jim: And life is just beginning for you. I believe you are an example of the kind of life David spoke about in Psalm 91: If you dwell in the shelter of the Most High, David says, you will find rest, because He is your refuge. He will command His angels to guard you in all your ways. You know, it seems to me that His angels were guarding you, or at least they were guarding Rosie when part of you was angry at her!

And here is another thing in this psalm which seems to fit you: David knew that the serpent symbolizes Satan, who struck fear into people's hearts, but the promise in this psalm, Keltie, is coming true for you. It says that *you* will trample the serpent! Although you were made silent through the curses of Satan, you now loudly proclaim the truth. I believe that every time you work for the Lord these days, you are trampling the serpent.

Then the psalm concludes by saying that the Lord will rescue those who love Him, will deliver them from trouble, and will *satisfy* them. That sounds like it is your story.

15

SPLENDID PEOPLE

THIS IS A good time to revise the way we think about "Multiple Personality." The incidence is turning out to be much higher than anyone expected. The number of MPD therapists is lagging far behind the growing demand, and since many therapists will be learning to treat it in the months ahead, those now in training should bypass the stereotypic way of viewing it. The things we are learning now need to be incorporated into the mainstream of clinical practice. It may make all the difference in the world to the clients, since any prejudicial blindness could send therapy into harmful directions.

The contributors to this book may not seem to be representative of multiples in general because they have received treatment which included a Christian perspective. But they are no different from other multiples, despite the differences in therapy. What is true about them as human beings is true about any survivor: Their suffering can come to an end.

The distinctive thing about the subjects of this study is that they have been adopted into the family of God, and are taking on the likeness of that family. My observations may therefore seem to apply only to multiples who are Christians, but I sense broader implications. We are all created in the image of God, and are welcome in His family. What is true for any could be true for all. Here are some things I have learned during this project. I hope they will promote better understanding and more effective treatment.

THESE PEOPLE BEAR
THE FAMILY RESEMBLANCE
OF THEIR HEAVENLY FATHER

A controversy was aired on a radio talk show this week, and it sent one of my clients into a suicidal episode. She is just beginning therapy with me, after believing for a long time that her personalities were demons, because of the different sound of their voices. One of the personalities in particular was very troubled, and she telephoned to tell me that she couldn't stop cutting her wrists. After hearing my first book belittled on the radio, she had lost confidence in me. She was afraid she was going to be labeled a demon again, even though I had taught her family and her other personalities that she is not. The problem is not demonization, and to call a personality a demon is nothing other than religious abuse. The talk show was one of those open forums, and the host took the point of view that there is no such thing as MPD—the "real problem" was said to be demons.

One caller asked if it was safe to let a person in her church, who was known to be a multiple, teach a children's Sunday school class. The radio show's host is said to have come down firmly with a negative answer—no multiples are to teach Sunday school. They have demons. Now what that did to my client was terrible—she is a wonderful Christian, loves God a lot, and has been heavily involved in her church for many years. The message to her was that she no longer belongs in church. Not only is she back to where she believes her parts are demons—that is bad enough—but now her community of friendships is also seriously threatened. If they find I have discovered her dissociative condition, they may abandon her, at least if they listened to the wrong talk show.

That is an example of how outdated thinking can send people to the brink of death. I am not so much concerned about the outdated thinking as I am concerned about people. It is time to recognize multiples as splendid people who have suffered. It is time to get a grip on fear, and to affirm these people as having a rightful place in God's family. In the case of my client, her identity has been "in Christ," and the family resemblance is hard to miss. She has had problems in living—dissociation kinds of problems—but she is doing the best she can, and she belongs in the family of God.

People often say about a young boy, "He sure looks like his father. He even *acts* the same." In some cases, the family image is easy to spot. That is the way it should be in God's family, and that is what I have found while talking with these people.

One of Jesus' teachings that illustrates this is where He tells His followers to be "perfect." It is actually a call for His disciples to be more like their heavenly Father. Here is that passage:

> You have heard that it was said, "Love your neighbor and hate your enemy." But I tell you: Love your enemies and pray for those who persecute you, that you may be sons of your Father in heaven. He causes his sun to rise on the evil and the good, and sends rain on the righteous and the unrighteous. If you love those who love you, what reward will you get? Are not even the tax collectors doing that? And if you greet only your brothers, what are you doing more than others? Do not even pagans do that? Be perfect, therefore, as your heavenly Father is perfect (Matthew 5:43-48, NIV).

Jesus portrays the Father here as one who bestows His blessings on everyone, without restriction. Not only does He cause the sun to rise on the "righteous" and the "unrighteous" alike, but He also sends the nourishing rain for the well-being of both groups. His care is bountiful for all people. His kindness is extended to everybody. That is the identity His children are supposed to grow up into.

It is the English word *perfect* that tends to mislead people when they look at this passage. It looks like we are being asked to "do everything right," like God. But the translation of the Greek word *perfect,* means "complete," so the teaching comes into focus like this:

> If you want to bear the likeness of the Father,
>   you should not go only half of the way
>   in showing good will.
> Go all the way—be complete ("perfect")
>   in your acts of kindness,
>   and don't leave out your enemies.
> You are to be generous to everybody.

One of the things that deeply impressed me about the people in this book as I reviewed our conversations is the lack of malice they express toward those who have hurt them. They are not eaten up with vengeful feelings. Although their suffering has been immense, they did not dream of turning the tables on their offenders. I am amazed at their desire to be understanding and kind to everybody. They are consumed with compassion. They display the family resemblance—not the kind which comes from their family of origin, but from their true family. Newheart wants to establish a safe house for survivors. Elizabeth wants to create a safer society, where healing will be promoted. Willie makes dolls to be used by therapists so they can work with survivors more effectively. Rick wants to create support networks for survivors in churches. Crystal wants to work in her church nursery, to show babies love. Christina helps people as they face death. Paula and Keltie enjoy being involved with groups of people, in the service of God. Meribeth eagerly awaits the arrival of her first baby, and the domestic joy that will bring.

Without exception, these people have turned their allegiance over to God, and have been transformed. From their staggering childhood pain has come strength. Their healing has been profound, and so has their joy. They want to act like their Father.

A LITTLE STIGMA HURTS A LOT

One repeated theme in the conversations was the power that *public stigma* has over the survivors. It is generally a disgrace even to be a *former* multiple. Elizabeth has spoken to quite a few groups, having been introduced as a multiple, and she explained to me how she has come to view things: People fear what they don't know. When they get to know her, and when they can discern that she is a solid person, their fear subsides. The need to stigmatize her also subsides. I hope understanding will spread and the stigmatization will decrease as she and others stay in the public spotlight.

There is a second kind of stigmatization that is more difficult to spot than the public one—the kind displayed by some therapists and "rescuers." Support and encouragement from friends and relatives are a vital part of a recovery program, but when much attention is paid to the valiant role of the rescuer, the rescuee must continue to stay unhealthy, or at least be displayed as unhealthy. That is stigmatizing.

Some of the conversations highlighted this problem for me. Therapists can adopt a kind of "one-up" position. They may be entirely unaware of this, but it keeps their MPD clients from growing. It carries the subtle message: "You need me. You are not healthy, and my position as your healthy partner will be necessary for a long time." That stigma is tough to pick up; it is usually first noticed by the multiple, who says, "Something is going wrong with the therapy these days."

The therapist can "interpret" that remark this way: "You are fighting me. I am to be the one in charge here. *You* must be stuck."

Maybe the therapist is the stuck one. If the therapist would encourage the multiple to live life from the adult personalities, and focus on getting a sense of teamwork among them all, things would probably get unstuck. I don't like to blame clients when therapy stalls—they are doing the best they can.

This subtle kind of stigma has even been heard to fall from the lips of well known seminar presenters. Their "off the record" comments reveal their positions. At one MPD conference, I sensed that the speaker who preceded me was a wonderful person, although I had not heard her presentation. Here is part of a conference evaluation that was mailed to me afterward:

> I really enjoyed the second workshop, when Dr. Friesen stepped in and let those of us who are multiples feel like *people*, and not like the fungus we seem to be in the other presenter's eyes.
>
> In Christ, there should be unconditional love and acceptance for those of us who have survived the horrors described in this workshop. We will also survive, and pray for, the poor 'unfortunates' who have been 'called' to work with us (by accident).
>
> I realize there can be much debate about whether or not to accept MPD. The most important thing is to accept the person, and let the Lord lead in the 'handling' of the problem. We all are just people who love the Lord, and had no choice in what we suffered.

Thank you, Dr. Friesen, for saying that we are worthwhile people. [To the first presenter] *If* God is leading you to work with this 'plague', I will be praying for understanding and direction for you. Your insights were very helpful, but the acceptance by Dr. Friesen was healing.

Please keep in mind that the other presenter is a wonderful person—a giving person. The above indicates, however, that she sends out the message that working with MPD is a sacrifice. If that is true for her, she should probably try something she enjoys, or she should start appreciating her MPD clients. Maybe some therapists hope that if they do their job well, the client will climb up to be a "normal" person. That is not the way I see them: I want them to be themselves, and most often they turn out to be quite a bit above "normal."

Some accounts have related how difficult MPD is to work with, and how "resistant" the clients are to therapy. My sense is that we need to re-examine what makes the clients resistant. Part of it is when the therapist sees himself as a "rescuer." That makes the position of the therapist more important than the position of the client—*the therapist needs to stay "one-up."*

When the therapist says, "I need to rescue you," the client stays unhealthy. The stigma is being reinforced. The need to stay hidden remains. The stereotype is strengthened, and the therapist's position proves to prophesy the outcome. It *does* take a long time for a multiple to get healthy when the therapist's position is at stake, but it is not because the client is "resistant"—it is because the stigma stirs up the client's lifelong feelings of shame and humiliation.

Not only does the stigma hurt a lot, but it also keeps the multiple in a "one-down" position. The point is, the stigma is a major obstacle—an unnecessary one. Progress can speed up a lot when the client's true worth is affirmed by everyone around.

CAPTIVES ARE BEING SET FREE

There are a lot of skirmishes on the road to mental health. It seems that as soon as one conflict has been taken care of properly, another one takes its place. There seems to be precious little time to enjoy the victory—another battle is on the horizon.

Here is an account which illustrates not only how hard these clients are willing to work, but also how hard the work is. This battle in my office was a quiet one—not even evident to me at the time—but it released Mary's child parts to accept Jesus into their hearts, and that victory helped her stay on the right path.

Mary started treatment with me to augment her on-going therapy with another therapist. Her child alters were highly fragile, and I wanted them to receive healing for whatever they had been through. I had no idea what their issues were—only that something was keeping them from treatment. The "kids," as Mary referred to them, did not rotate out and talk to me. On the surface of it, the issue was safety—they needed to be protected. I asked them to do some drawing. This allowed me access to one of the child parts whose artwork showed it could not get past the notion that it was "bad." I said that its drawing shows the child believes it is "badder than all the bad people." The following is transcribed from the tape recording of this session.

* * *

Mary: [She is speaking here from an adult personality, who is looking at the artwork just completed by the child part.] I can understand that. I really can understand how a child would think that. But I don't know what to do about it, and no amount of logic convinces it. There is nothing I can do to change that one's mind.

Jim: Yes—it's not logic that helps kids anyway.

Mary: Oh, it isn't? What does?

Jim: Understanding, love, comfort, encouragement, healing. If the kids feel they are bad, that's not the way for them to get healthy. They have to be adored, like children deserve.

Mary: That concept is really hard to get ahold of.

Jim: Okay, let's try something. Try to see a house that is you, and all of your characters are there. Everything there is you. A conference area is a good thing to have in the house, where anybody can come for open discussions. They can leave if they want, and they can come back in. And there's an intercom system so that everybody can hear what's going on.

Mary: Oh, that's good, so if anybody doesn't want to show up, they can still hear.

Jim: Right. Everybody will be able to hear everything. So let's go to that house.

Mary: Okay. I've got one.

Jim: Let's go over to the conference area, and I would like to speak on the intercom, and help people understand a couple of basic things, okay?

Mary: The kids you want to talk to are sitting on the floor—with no intercom.

Jim: Okay. The ones that are here can hear me, and the ones that are choosing to stay in their rooms can hear me, too, because they've got the intercom. And this is a real neat message, because it's Jesus' message [reading from Matthew 19:13,14]:

> Some people brought children to Jesus for him to place his hands on them and pray. But the disciples scolded those people. Jesus said, "Let the children come to me and do not stop them, because the kingdom of Heaven belongs to such as these." And He placed his hands on them and blessed them.

People didn't appreciate children as much as they should. Jesus saw that, didn't He? Jesus loves children.

Mary: Your words are going by too fast.

Jim: Okay. Do you want me to read it again? ("Yes.") I'm going to read it from a different section of the Bible, okay? Jesus said some things that were mentioned in different parts of the Bible. Matthew, Mark, Luke and John kind of summarize the teachings of Jesus. What I just read to you was from Matthew. This is what Luke said, in about the same way:

> Some people brought their babies to Jesus to have him place his hands on them. But the disciples saw them and scolded them for doing so.

Mary: [Interrupting.] But why?

Jim: Well, they didn't appreciate kids very much.

Mary: Why not?

Jim: I don't know. Here's what it says:

> Jesus called the children to him and said, "Let the children come to me. Do not stop them, because the kingdom of God

belongs to such as these. Remember this, whoever does not receive the kingdom of God like a child will never enter it."

Mary: What is *it?*

Jim: The kingdom of God.

Mary: What's that?

Jim: All the people that are God's children in the whole world. I am a child of God. He's adopted me and he's adopted you, too. The problem in this story is that the adults thought kids weren't important enough to bring to Jesus. But Jesus knew better. He said, "Bring them to me! Don't stop them from coming to me!" Jesus knew how important kids are. Isn't that beautiful?

Mary: There's too many big words.

Jim: Jesus loves children. Do they understand that?

Mary: No.

Jim: He loves them, and people who love Jesus protect and take care of children.

Mary: They do?

Jim: He wants to protect them, and not let anybody hurt them.

Mary: Maybe He will change his mind.

Jim: He is God, and cannot change His mind.

Mary: What if they're bad kids?

Jim: Who says kids are bad?

Mary: [Moaning] Everybody, I guess.

Jim: Invite Jesus into the conference room so you can ask Him what He thinks about kids.

Mary: Somebody won't let me listen to Him. Somebody is trying to tear me away from Him. Somebody is grabbing and pulling me away from Him and shouting over his words.

Jim: Who are you, shouting above Jesus' words?

Mary: It feels like my mother.

Jim: Please be silent. Jesus said not to cause little children to stumble, so you'd better not do that. You'd better listen to Him.

Mary: They are afraid.

Jim: He has some important things to say about kids, so go ahead, Jesus.

Mary: [Silence for twenty seconds.] It's too impossible to believe. [Almost crying] I'm afraid it will go away tomorrow.

Jim: What did He say?

Mary: He picked up the one, put her on His lap and hugged her, and then carried her over and sat on the floor with the rest of them. He said, "You're okay." But He hasn't said anything to all the ones on the floor. They won't understand anyway.

Jim: Let them listen. I think they can understand Him.

Mary: I don't think so.

Jim: Give Him a chance.

Mary: [Silence for thirty seconds.] No, He's not talking. He's putting His hands on this one's head and that one's cheek, and they're scooting closer.

* * *

The tape recording of our session stopped there, but this is what she told her other therapist in a recording of their next session.

Mary: Dr. Friesen wanted to talk to the part he'd made sit down in the chair and be quiet. He wanted to talk to that part, but that part was furious at him. And it wouldn't talk to him. I could feel it wanting to strangle him. It looked like it had a body, but I couldn't see any face. It was definitely older—an adult. I don't know what it was. It wasn't a child, but it was smaller than an adult. It was talking so loudly that you couldn't hear anything else, and it was saying things like, "Stay away from Jesus. He's not safe. This isn't real." He wanted to strangle Dr. Friesen.

I told Dr. Friesen what I was feeling, and he said, "Okay, let's let Jesus talk to this part."

And I saw Jesus get up off the floor leaving the children there, and I thought He was going to go over and talk to the part, but no way! He walked around the conference table to the back, behind this part. And he put his hands on its shoulders. And I thought, "Nice. He's going to touch this part while He's talking to it." And the part just started screaming and shrieking. I could sense that this part was feeling burned by Jesus' hands, but I couldn't feel it. Jesus held on to its shoulders while it screamed and screeched, and then Jesus just picked it up by the shoulders and threw it in a lake. Dr. Friesen read the Scriptures over to the kids again, and they understood them and were happy.

Mary: [Two weeks later in the other therapist's office.] I was sitting in church yesterday, and I didn't hear the whole first three quarters of the sermon. I don't know where I was, but I didn't hear any of it. I felt that the kids were listening, and I knew it at the time. There was a manger scene, and they were gathered all around it. And the kids were responding, but not with surface emotions. Some deep level underneath was stirred up. I heard a little voice say, "You know what? No baby ever hurt anybody." And there was an understanding that it was okay to open up and let Him in, because no baby ever hurt anybody.

The sermon wasn't that great or anything. But later on I thought, "There's no trouble." Here is this baby in the manger, and all these little children around it saying he can't hurt us. He's come to bring peace that lasts for a whole lifetime. And on the way home I was thinking, "No, it's not trouble." There was no pain. When these kids were opening up to this baby, there was no pain. And then when I got home, I thought, "Did it have anything to do with what Dr. Friesen said about Jesus throwing the part that wouldn't let the children hear the Scriptures into the lake? Did that have anything to do with it?" There was a significant religious experience for the kids at church yesterday.

* * *

Mary told me everything the next time we met, and she was filled with joy. She maintains that ever since Jesus threw that thing into the lake, which we believe was a demon, her "kids" have been growing, and loving life.

The word *freedom* has come up repeatedly while researching for this book. No background can keep people trapped. Prayers to be freed from suffering are answered, as Jesus taught: "Ask and it will be given to you; seek and you will find; knock and the door will be opened to you" (Luke 11:9). Those promises have been kept. Jesus announced the purpose of His ministry this way: He has come to set the captives free (Luke 4:18).

LOVE IS MORE POWERFUL THAN FEAR

We all know about the bad-apple effect, even if we have not actually seen how a rotten one can spoil a perfectly good barrel of fruit. These people have reported a different kind of influence, the "ripple effect." When remarkably wonderful things happen, it clearly helps more than just one person, and has a broadening positive effect as well. Abundant life spreads, much like a ripple. It will cover the whole pond if there is no obstruction.

In *Uncovering the Mystery of MPD*, I reported that churches which get involved in the lives of survivors find that they grow and that their people reach greater spiritual depths. I continue to find this to be true. This book highlights certain clients' stories and lessons, and although other people could have been included, these survivors' lives illustrate that many of them have became MORE THAN SURVIVORS.

Those who have learned to know these people have been forced to grow, too, and to think in new ways. I want to speak for myself at this point. Some of the most thrilling moments of my life were when my children were born. I was present and involved, and I helped with their births—and my exhilaration lasted for a long time. That was joy, on a grand scale. I have had that same kind of experience, although at a lower level, with these clients. It is almost as though, in some way, they have been reborn. Although many sessions are rather subdued and somewhat draining, there is still a certain amount of light-heartedness and levity. But when conflicts are resolved, when wounds receive long-awaited healing, a steady stream of joy fills the room.

I was once called on to provide therapy for a person who was newly released from prison, and *she could not stop saying what a relief it was to be out.* Her life had *ceased* for the weeks of her incarceration. She could not eat; she was constantly ill and totally depressed; and she was terrorized by fellow inmates. But the minute she was released, it was life anew for her.

That is what a therapy session can seem like when a demonized child alter, who has known only abuse and terror, is freed. When those horrifying experiences are replaced with God's love, it is a brand new world. That kind of life-changing transformation absolutely *must* infect those around with joy. I think it is almost like what Mr. Scrooge went through on Christmas morning: He had come face to face with his own death, and he lived to see a sparkling new day—one filled with the people he loved. That kind of spiritual lift comes from God, and it spreads. Satan may foist death and destruction on his followers as something they are supposed to value, but the love that comes from God is the genuine article—transparently valuable.

A NEW STEREOTYPE IS NEEDED

My hunch about multiples found a lot of support as I gathered this material. I did not put out a public announcement that I was looking for volunteers, but of the nine people featured, I had specifically sought out only the two I knew—Crystal and Willie Marie. Each of the other seven were people I had heard about from their friends or therapists. In the cases of Christina and Elizabeth, I met them at a conference. I think these nine represent multiples quite accurately. They show the characteristics that I have seen many times. There are multiples I did not interview, whose lives have been shattered into more pieces, or some whose course of treatment may have taken different pathways, but I believe these are representative of people who dissociate.

Actually, if I had tried, I could have looked up doctors, executives, professors, and a few other highly visible dissociative people to interview, but that did not seem right. I could wrongly indicate that achievement is the only important measure of success. Nonetheless, it is clear that, athough they don't want it known, many highly successful people dissociate. That statement leads to the conclusion that we really do need a new stereotype so the picture of MPD will better reflect what is becoming evident: These people have a lot to offer.

Characteristics

They are gifted people, compassionate people, who want to get healthy. Their natural abilities are recognized more and more these days, as multiples and former multiples are encouraged to display them. It used to be that when a seminar presenter would show remarkable MPD artwork at a convention, the implied message was, "Well, now. Here is one that is talented. Isn't that amazing?"

Yes, it is amazing—but *many* of them are talented. Actually, it is unusual to find one who isn't.

They are overcomers. They are splendid people. They have suffered greatly, but they are strong. The "more than survivors" factor is that not only are they strong, but they also have a lot of compassion. One would expect them to turn out calloused and cold, but they are people of love.

They don't deceive and manipulate, as some people—even therapists—have suggested. Those occurrences are the result of confusion and a sense of lack of safety, but they ardently seek health and truth. When given safe housing and an environment in which to flourish, they are decidedly cooperative in treatment, even when they encounter difficult feelings.

TREATMENT IMPLICATIONS

The simple model of treating multiple personalities "one on one" in individual therapy has its limits. A multiple also needs to associate with a number of informed, supportive people. When these people are included in the therapy, the multiple is more apt to live most of his (or her) life in his healthiest personalities, making wiser choices and feeling more successful. Multiples do their best as part of a community.

Rick shows a good understanding about what it is going to take to work with the many multiples who do not yet have therapists. I like his vision, where people in the church become knowledgeable and trained well enough to keep misunderstanding at a minimum while treatment is underway. Elizabeth has a similar vision: Accurate information about MPD should be widely disseminated. That will help everybody—especially the multiples. Her workbooks are designed to teach multiples how to seek the greatest good for all of the selves.

Rick and Elizabeth know about MPD from the inside, and they place a high value on the participation of the family and the community in restoration. Both also see the place for a therapist—in doing memory work, unravelling the tangles of amnesia, and working through obstacles. It seems to me that the therapist can concentrate on those things, and friends can be the ones who promote growth and development.

A TWO-PART MODEL

The following two-part model appears to have a lot of utility, particularly if the supply of dissociation-experienced therapists continues to be insufficient. It emphasizes developing healthy relationships in the real world, and allows therapists to become effectively involved with a high number of multiple clients. The model assumes that we are not viewing this as a disease, and that we highly esteem those who have grown up with it. Family and friends are viewed as members of the community who are the multiples' peers—a community where stigma and shame are not active. They assume these people are to be enjoyed, at whatever point in therapy they may be. Contrary to the popular perception, these people are enriching to know.

Part One: Guidelines for Creating a Safety Network

Included here are guidelines for developing an enriching living environment for multiple clients. This is where the restoration needs to begin. If there is no safe, understanding group of people who can support what goes on in treatment, it will be seriously undermined. Getting established and learning to live life daily is the place to start. The daily routine needs to be socially enhancing, and needs to encourage the expression of talents. Therapy needs to address itself to this part of the model first, before the second part.

Multiples often wish to get on to the memory work before family and friends are ready to support it, but that can lead to divisions and disagreements. Dissociating clients need to avoid confrontations, because when the family says one thing and the therapist says another, despair is bound to set in. The therapist and the network need to have a good working relationship.

These guidelines do not follow any particular order. It is good to keep them all in mind. When things go wrong, any of them could be slipping.

1. *Therapists need to specialize in this area.* They should create or join an MPD team, and join the International Society for the

Study of Multiple Personality & Dissociation, by calling (708) 966-4322. The ISSMP&D is the only organization to date that is forging ahead with treatment issues. Academic institutions are making little or no headway in understanding MPD, nor in training therapists to work with related problems. Therapists need to seek training and supervision, and then keep learning as long as they continue to treat this condition.

2. *Promoting safety in the client's environment must be the top priority.* If the dissociator is "on the alert" for signs of impending danger, the traumatized parts will be inaccessible to treatment. The therapist needs to assess the safety factor in the home environment before sharing the diagnosis, and keep updating the network with helpful information.

"Living life to the fullest" includes being part of an enriching community. There is a high possibility that without the proper environmental support and safety, the personalities will become disoriented, as the system is getting reorganized early in treatment. It is very helpful when a friend or family member can act as a central contact person, to go between the therapist and the network people. When possible, this person should attend all or most of the therapy sessions. This deters misunderstandings and spreads therapeutic conditions to the home.

3. *Confrontation should be eliminated from therapy and from the home environment.* Confrontation often engages a defending personality, which puts the hurt child alters into hiding. To prepare the client for the difficult parts of therapy, the therapist needs to befriend the defending personalities, so they can help with reorganizing the system. They are the ones who will allow the hurt child alters to surface for healing, which will not happen in the presence of a confronting therapist or confronting friends.

4. *Provide hope and faith, but avoid minimizing feelings.* These clients have had their feelings discounted in every way imaginable throughout the years, and that needs to be stopped. They have very painful feelings, and those need to be validated. The hope and faith come about when the therapist and others praise the qualities they are observing in the client. After a difficult feeling has been opened up, it is important to avoid saying, "I know things will be getting better for you soon." That

is not an expression of faith in the client. That is minimization. It would be much better to state that the client is showing a lot of courage in working with the difficult feelings.

From my vantage point, it seems that most "12-step" programs are not effective in helping dissociators. They often provide a generalized hope that if certain steps are followed, life will be better. That approach is good in some ways, but it does not validate the depth of suffering that these people have gone through, and it does not tie the hope for improvement directly to the person's gifts. Another problem with 12-stepping is that it tends to keep dissociators in a "one-down" position, as though recovery should not ever be expected to come to an end point. "I will always be recovering" is not the way to approach these people. That is not a faith-inducing idea. That is a medical idea, which may be appropriate for chemical addictions but certainly does not fit dissociators. They need to know there will be an end to their suffering.

5. *Teach the client to live life from the strong selves, and reserve work with the injured selves to be carried out in therapy or in specified settings.* Friends can encourage this approach, particularly if they have been included in some of the therapy sessions. Get every self to work for the common good. That usually means having the adult selves stay in charge most of the time, while the child selves are safely kept away from the stresses of adult living. Train MPDs to use dissociation positively—for personal benefit. They can negotiate with intrusive thoughts and feelings to wait until later when their issues can be attended to more effectively. One possible cause of continuing instability can be danger in the home. Protective personalities may detect the danger, but are unable to talk about it. Even when therapy is safe, it may be difficult to open up about major threats at home, which keeps things unstable in both places. In cases where flashbacks and frequent switching keep things unstable, antidepressant medication can be helpful.

6. *Resist the urge to rush to the end of therapy.* This is a common mistake. Of course, we all want to bring as much healing as quickly as possible, and we all want to make life as livable as possible, but rushing does not help. The key is not getting

finished with therapy ASAP, but enjoying life each day. Keep in mind that life is for living, and although difficult feelings are certain to be encountered, it is *life* that goes on, not *feelings*. Resist the multiple's desire to be "integrated" too soon. The goal is healing, not integrating. Concentrate on healing, and concentrate on living. Do a thorough job, not a quick one.

7. *Include spiritual dimensions of healing.* Sometimes there is no willingness to work for the selves' common good until there is spiritual accord. As Jesus said, "A man cannot serve two masters." The rift between a group of Christian alters and a group with other loyalties needs to be overcome. The wounded, misled alters can use their strength to further God's kingdom after they have received His healing. When God is in the middle of the system, it is much easier for all the selves to work for their common good. Their allegiance to Him and to His family creates health and safety.

When there is a church or a Christian network, prayer is important. Breakthroughs have resulted not only from intercessory prayer, but also from prayer for the healing of memories, and from exorcism/deliverance. When exorcism is practiced, it is to be carried out by people with experience in both the Christian and the psychological arenas. Distinguishing between selves and demons is crucial, which is more fully addressed in *Uncovering the Mystery of MPD*. Whenever personality parts are identified as demons, and subjected to exorcism, serious harm is done. That is religious abuse. Nonetheless, after seeking the Lord's leading, marvelous breakthroughs often result from exorcisms. Captive selves can be set free.

Part Two: Healing, Unity and Obstacles

If the client is properly supported and stability has been established in the system, the time in therapy can be directed to healing and to connecting the personality states. Healing often needs to be directed to particular traumatic events, or to some of the injured selves, as part of the stabilization process. But the objective is getting the client to live in the healthy selves. When a healthy living routine is established, *then* therapy can turn to the systematic healing of memories and to unity.

8. *Do not make therapy more complicated than it needs to be.* Therapy progresses best when it is simple and straight forward. Avoid using confusing terminology.

"Integration" happens throughout therapy, whenever the selves get to know things about each other. Any sharing of thoughts, feelings or wishes is an integrative process. "Fusion" is a word that has been used to describe the point where alter personalities become united, but the integrative process is not finished right then—memories, thoughts, sensations, and lots of ideas continue to get hooked up for weeks after the point of unity has been passed. In therapy, use words that keep things workable: merge, join, coalesce, cluster, and unity. Ideas do not have to get any more complex than that.

9. *Plan interventions to promote connectedness.* Explore journaling and artwork, and anything else that increases sharing between the personality states. Some activities work for certain people, but not for others. Find the most productive methods of closing the distance between the selves for each client.

10. *Talk about obstacles, and promote healing for the traumas from which they have sprung.* Many times the obstacles that threaten to end treatment—despair, helplessness, hopelessness, abandonment, suicide and rage, to name a few—are the outward expressions of feelings that have their origin in a traumatic memory. For example, an intense fear of abandonment may appear in an otherwise healthy relationship, and is traceable to being buried during a ritual. The fear is not going to dissipate until the ritual memory receives healing. Those obstacles require careful handling in the therapy session, and require aftercare in the living environment.

11. *Spiritual healing is vital.* Lots of traumas have definite spiritual implications, which need attention. These traumas include death rituals and sexual abuse. Child personalities need to be released from fear, and if demons have been included in the traumatic events, the spiritual abuse and aftereffects need to be dealt with. The demonic needs to be expelled as part of the healing process. Unity is not difficult after spiritual needs have been attended to.

FITTING THE DIAGNOSIS TO THE CONDITION

"Multiple personality disorder," as a term, has gathered a lot of baggage. Peoples' preconceptions tend to be firmly in place, and many times they completely overlook the talents of multiple personality clients. There are two other problems with the term: (1) It puts too much emphasis on outward appearances (switching); and, (2) it does not direct attention to healing.

Other diagnostic terms have been suggested to replace the present one, including chronic traumatic disorder, and post-traumatic stress disorder—chronic. Those have their problems as well. To suggest that things are "chronic" is to prophecy failure in treatment. Maybe things are difficult, but when spiritual issues are included in treatment, and when a safety network is in place, the outcome is bright—certainly not chronic. I offer the following diagnostic terms for rotating personality systems, and for other types of dissociation. They direct attention to the needed healing, and identify the dividedness that needs to be dealt with:

POST-TRAUMATIC STRESS DISORDER,
WITH ALTERNATING PERSONALITY STATES
and
POST-TRAUMATIC STRESS DISORDER,
WITH PARTIALLY CONNECTED PERSONALITY STATES.

Both these conditions can exist simultaneously
for a given individual.

These diagnoses rise above implications that these people are doomed to be low-functioning folks. It allows that they have been through suffering but have retained their natural abilities by disconnecting from the pain. It properly directs attention to the healing of memories. It also permits us to view them as splendid people, because their ability to disconnect has helped them to become more than mere survivors.

REFERENCE NOTES

1. Anti*psychotic* medication has a slowing effect on brains. People with schizophrenia or other psychoses benefit from these chemicals. However, when antipsychotic medication is given to MPD clients, there is no benefit, and sometimes the slowing effect is quite detrimental. The switching does not work as well, and since that is their best coping skill, when it is taken away from them they flounder. On the other hand, the anti*depressant* drugs are often beneficial for multiples while they are in the most difficult part of treatment, the memory retrievals, which are accompanied by highly charged emotions. Antidepressant drugs produce increased tolerance to stress, which is exactly what multiples need during treatment.

2. For a fuller explanation, see *Uncovering the Mystery of MPD,* chapter 4.

3. Studies keep coming up with the same results — practically all MPD starts out in childhood, most often during the preschool years, and 80 to 90 percent of the time it is found to be the result of sexual abuse. It is horrifying to the survivors, but because most of the time the abuse cannot be verified, many survivors find it more practical to avoid telling their story in public. Public disclosure would likely pull a lot of denial and hostility from the perpetrator(s), so the choice is usually made to avoid further chaos by keeping quiet.

4. "Eve," in *Three Faces of Eve* (her name is Chris Sizemore), has gone public with her story. Her books, including *A Mind of My Own,* are stellar examples of how a woman who has suffered has been able to help so many others. Another person whose extreme abuse (SRA) led her to go public with her story is Michelle Smith, in *Michelle Remembers.* One other MPD/SRA survivor, whose identity is protected, tells her story in *Suffer the Child.* Robert Meyer, a therapist, has portrayed the lives and the therapy of many SRA survivors in *Satan's Children.* (That certainly would not be a title I would choose!)

SUGGESTED READING LIST

Blume, E. Sue. *Secret Survivors: Uncovering Incest and Its Aftereffects in Women.* New York: Ballantine Books, 1990.

Cohen, Barry M.; Giller, Esther; and Lynn, W., editors. *Multiple Personality Disorder From the Inside Out.* Baltimore, MD: Sidran Press, 1991.

Friesen, James G. *Uncovering the Mystery of Multiple Personality Disorder.* San Bernardino, CA: Here's Life Publishers, 1991.

Isaacs, T. Craig. *The Possessive States Disorder: The Differentiation of Involuntary Spirit-Possession From Present Diagnostic Categories.* Ann Arbor, MI: University Microfilms, 1985.

Koch, Kurt. *Christian Counselling and Occultism.* Grand Rapids: Kregel Publications, 1972.

Kraft, Charles H. *Christianity With Power: Discovering the Truth About Signs and Wonders.* Ann Arbor, MI: Servant Publications, 1989.

Los Angeles County Commission for Women. "Ritual Abuse: Definitions, Glossary, the Use of Mind Control," 1989. Phone (310) 974-1455.

Maltz, Wendy. *The Sexual Healing Journey: A Guide for Survivors of Sexual Abuse.* New York: Harper Collins Publishers, 1991.

Power, Elizabeth. *Managing Our Selves: Building a Community of Caring,* 1992.
E. Power & Associates
P. O. Box 2346
Brentwood, TN 37024-2346
Phone (615) 327-1510

Ryder, Daniel. *Breaking the Circle of Satanic Ritualistic Abuse: Recognizing and Recovering From the Hidden Trauma.* Minneapolis, MN: CompCare Publishers, 1992.

Swissler, Mary Ann. *Deliverance From Evil: Survivors of Ritualistic Abuse Speak Out.* Pasadena CA: Pasadena Publishing Co. (P. O. Box 60421, Pasadena, CA 91116-1992.

Wagner, C. Peter, and Pennoyer, F. Douglas, editors. *Wrestling With Dark Angels: Toward a Deeper Understanding of the Supernatural Forces in Spiritual Warfare.* Ventura, CA: Regal Books, 1990.

White, Thomas B. *The Believer's Guide to Spiritual Warfare.* Ann Arbor, MI: Servant Publications, 1990.

Wilder, E. James. *A Redemptive Response to Satanism.* InterVarsity Press. (In process.)